Helion & Company Limited
Unit 8 Amherst Business Centre
Budbrooke Road
Warwick
CV34 5WE
England
Tel. 01926 499 619
Email: info@helion.co.uk
Website: www.helion.co.uk
Twitter: @helionbooks
Visit our blog https://helionbooks.wordpress.com/

Typeset by Oliver Barstow, Milan, Italy
Cover design by Paul Hewitt, Battlefield Design (www.battlefield-design.co.uk)

ISBN 978-1-804515-72-3

British Library Cataloguing-in-Publication Data
A catalogue record for this book is available from the British Library

CONTENTS

Note: In order to simplify the use of this book, all names, locations and geographic designations are as provided in *The Times World Atlas*, or other traditionally accepted major sources of reference, as of the time of described events.

ABBREVIATIONS AND ACRONYMS

AMIS	African Union Mission in Sudan (AU peacekeeping force deployed primarily in Darfur)
AMIS II	African Union Mission in Sudan, expanded operation
AMIS III	African Union Mission in Sudan, final expansion
AU	African Union
DITF	Darfur Integrated Task Force
EU	European Union
JEM	Justice and Equality Movement
JLOC	Joint Logistics Operations Centre
NATO	North Atlantic Treaty Organization
NGO	non-governmental organisation
PAE	Pacific Architects and Engineers (US defence and government service contractor)
SLA	Sudan Liberation Army (armed wing of the SLM)
SLM	Sudan Liberation Movement
SPLA	Sudanese People's Liberation Army (South Sudan)
UN	United Nations
UNAMID	United Nations-African Union Mission in Darfur
UNSC	United Nations Security Council

1 DARFUR

The geography and history of the Darfur region of Sudan requires very close attention from the researcher, as it is not always as easy to comprehend as it may appear. Darfur is a troubled region, which has long been the scene of ethnic and cultural division, and it has been so for a long time. Before turning to the description of the conflicts that have devastated the area, it is important to take a look at the land and history of the region in order to make it easier to understand the roots of the problems that have practically destroyed the land and the lives of the people living in it.

The etymology of Darfur comes from the Arabic term 'Dar Fur' which literally means 'the land of the Fur'. It is practically surrounded by Chad, Libya and South Sudan. The area at first seems small, but when we take a closer look at the size of the conflict-ridden territory, we come up with a surprising number: its area is 1,886,068km^2.[1] As Darfur is a region of Sudan, perhaps it is useful to define the length of its borders with the adjacent territories: to the north and the east it borders the Northern State (675km), Northern Kordofan (360km), and Southern Kordofan (515km).

Along these borders there are several conflicts which have also made it difficult for the authorities to cope with the problems of these troubled lands. For example, between Darfur and South Sudan there lies the Bahr al-Arab (or Kiir River), and its course is a scene of sorrow because of the proximity of the South Darfur region and the Western Bahr al-Ghazal (South Sudan), and there are problems between the Dinka people and the Arabs of Darfur who fight over ethno-cultural issues, as well as land and water.[2]

To the west, Darfur is bordered by Chad, and along with the present problems, the conflict there has its roots in British-French rivalry prevalent throughout colonial times, when the two areas were borderlands between the two superpowers at the time. Colonial heritage is an important issue in the history of the country, which is now independent and tries to survive on its own. Another problem is posed by the climatic conditions that set apart the two regions of Sudan: there is the northern, desert area, which is dry and usually short of rain, and to the south, is a somewhat tropical savanna climate which differs in much from the other territory. The main difference between the two regions is that in the northern part the desert climate requires the people living there to maintain a nomadic lifestyle, whereas in the southern part the majority of the residents are used to sedentary farming, and they do not migrate to follow their animals.[3]

The Darfur region can be divided into three separate entities, which differ from each other in their vegetation and the way people live there. The northern section consists mostly of people of African and Arabic descent who are used to herding camels and lead a nomadic life, while in the middle section mostly African residents tend to cultivate their farms in a more fertile climate, and lastly, in the southern area an Arabic population tries to survive by herding cattle and trying to live a half-nomad, half-settled life.

To understand better the history of Darfur, it is useful to know that it became an independent province in 1956, and it was essentially the same regional division as el-Fasher (which is now its 'capital'). However, it was not independent from its mother country, Sudan, and in 1970, administrative measures divided its territory into North and South Darfur with capitals at el-Fasher and Nyala. Nevertheless, the territorial division was not complete even after this, for in 1994 a further, third part emerged: besides North and South Darfur, West Darfur was established with its capital el-Geneina. With an arid climate, it was very clear that the camel and cattle herders and the settlers survive with very limited water sources, as there are no rivers in the area, and the only natural water that can be found is from wells which are not always reliable in the amount they can provide.

The mountains that characterise the Darfur region – the Jebel Marrah, with the highest point of the area reaching 3,088 meters – are mostly composed of volcanic stones and granite fields, and along with the desert give some colour to the terrain in the area.[4] Despite the low number of watercourses in the desert area that surrounds Darfur, there are some watersheds in the mountains which provide water for the indigenous shepherds or farmers, present here since ancient times, to enable their animals to drink and their plants to grow, and live an often prosperous life there.[5] Although the territory is arid and the desert and savannah are the common climate around Darfur, thanks to these mountainous rivers and wells the local residents are able to grow fruits and vegetables, among them pomaceous and citrus fruits, which are available for consumption and trade. Flora in the area consists of 900 varieties and are therefore a very useful commodity for those residing in the area.[6] There is also much fauna in the Jebel Marra area and many animals graze on the little fertile territory the Darfur region can provide for them, including addayes, gazelles, oryxes and kudu. The somewhat rich flora and fauna thus contribute to the special landscape of the mostly deserted and arid area and may come as a pleasant surprise to the intrepid traveller. The mountain rivers are however not the only sources of water that can satisfy the thirst of animals and people. There is a unique phenomenon in the area where there is usually desert: the wadis, which are usually empty, fill up when it rains, and supply the animals and people with drinkable water in the usually dry desert. When it rains, the wadis create alluvial plains where agriculture also becomes possible temporarily.[7]

Understanding the climate of the country is also important to obtaining a comprehensive picture of the Darfur region. The general distinctions between the climate zones can be given in concrete terms. To the north lies the desert area, which is very hot and the temperature can even reach 50 °C during the day. The wind is dry here and rain almost never falls, with as little as 100mm annually. Going to the south there is a semi-tropical area, with 100–250 mm of rainfall every year, which is still very little for animal husbandry and farming. The average temperature is however more moderate, reaching 20 °C each day. Further south is the savannah zone which can be either dry or wet, depending on the specific area. In this area, the temperature is so moderate that it allows the cultivation of some plants and even animal husbandry. It goes without saying that this part of Darfur has a special importance for the locals as they depend on the small amount of rain and arable area that exists in this part of the territory.

The flora of the Darfur region is well adapted to the climate zones described above. The northern part has desert and savanna-type vegetation, to which belongs several types of Acacia, Combretum and other kinds of trees. In the middle, where the climate is semi-arid, there are more trees, and grass is usually widespread across the area. When reaching the southern part, the tropical climate leads to a territory which is full of rainforests.[8] All in all, the Sub-Saharan region, to which Darfur belongs, is full of bushes and dry grass, which encompass the whole area, and thorny plants are also widespread across the semi-arid land.[9]

To understand better the background of the Darfur region and its tribal rivalries, it is also important to take a brief look at the economy of the area. The common animal husbandry and farming is complemented by the forestry that is conducted on a lower scale. However, agriculture has been affected by several issues, one of them being the civil wars that have devastated the countryside in Sudan.[10] Despite having little to cultivate in this area of the world, the Darfurians have not given up on agriculture and animal husbandry. They mostly grow peanuts, gum arabic, sorghum, millet, wheat and barley,[11] but they also care for animals and breed cattle, which is an activity of both the Arabic and the African populations. This was one reason for the ethnic conflicts in the area: herdsmen, who were mostly Arabic, needed to follow their animals as they found sources of drinking water, sometimes travelling hundreds of kilometres, thus coming into conflict with the sedentary farmer population, who were mainly of African descent. The nomadic people also breed goats and sheep, which give them milk and other types of goods that supplied them with food and helped their everyday survival in the harsh conditions imposed on them by the climate and the land.

The most important animals are the camels, which are a favourite of the Arabic tribes, used for transport as well as their meat and milk. The camel has also been a measure of property and wealth in desert and Arabic societies since ancient times, and thus the ownership of more animals meant that a person was more influential in the desert society.[12]

As the area is short of naturally occurring metals and oil, industry has been mostly neglected by the local people in favour of agriculture. However, production of edible oil, building and the leather industry are some areas in which the populace have acquired some mastery, and the handicraft of the desert people is worth mentioning.

Having described the basic geographical, climatic and land characteristics of the Darfur region, an understanding of the ethnic background of the people of that region will also prove useful in

A herder from one of the Zaghawa tribes watches over his camels. (János Besenyő)

understanding the unresolved conflicts that have existed for decades. Darfur's population is not particularly dense, there being some 7.4 million inhabitants. The most important languages relevant to this study are those of the Arabs, the Fur, the Masalit and the Zaghawa tribes.[13] To understand better the grievances that have occurred in the region over time, it is useful to take a closer look at each of these tribes to form an understanding of their customs and ethnic background in order to be able to distinguish between the different groupings.

The first of the major ethnic tribes to be examines are the Arabs,[14] who not only constitute part of Darfur but also live throughout the Middle East and North Africa. The majority of researchers share the opinion that the Arabs did not come to the area before the fifteenth century. They trace themselves to Abdallah al-Juhayni, the name-giver of their clan in the territory of Darfur. Other non-Arab tribes and empires of the area also highlight their alleged Arabic descendance or their relationship to the prophet Muhammad, but these are most likely to have been fabricated in order to vindicate claims to the right to rule the country. There are several groups of Arabs living in the area; the Baggara, who breed cattle; others include the Abbala or Jammala who herd camels. Another clan is called the Beni Hassan.

The second most important ethnic group in the area are the Fur people, who form non-Arab, black ethnic tribes.[15] The language of these two million people is not related to Arabic, and they mostly live near Jebel Marra (the mountain in the west). The most important feature of the Fur people is that they established the Sultanate of Darfur in the seventeenth and eighteenth centuries, which was the main force in the area until modern times.

After the Fur people, are the Mashalits, who originally lived in the western part of Darfur, near the Chadian border, but nowadays they live in the southern part near Querida.[16]

A man in el-Fasher. (János Besenyő)

A water-collecting point in el-Fasher. (János Besenyő)

Another important ethnic group in the area are the Zaghawa people, speakers of a Chadian language called Beri.[17] They – through intermarriage – entered into the power struggle in Darfur in the eighteenth and nineteenth centuries but were not as influential as the other tribes. They number around 600,000 people.[18]

Having identified the ethnic background of the tribes that comprise the Darfurian area, and their cultural-political affiliations, it is also important to consider the religion that is practiced throughout the region, which is of course Islam. The religion spread across the land in the sixteenth century, when preachers from religious centres arrived at the call of the sultans of the area and started their missionary work. The sedentary population converted rather easily, while the nomads were harder to break. Until the nineteenth century there were no organised Sufi teachings in the area, but then so-called *tariqas* (schools) developed in Africa, and in the Sudanese area the *Tijaniyya* became one of the most popular sects of the Sufi order.

History of the Darfur Area

In the beginning of recorded history, this area of Africa was inhabited mostly by people of local descent, and there were several tribes who created empires in the territory that influenced the beginnings of the area located in Western Sudan; the Kanem/Bornu, Wadai and Baguirmi empires. After these developments, around 2500 BC – and related to the drying out of the Sahara – there may have been an empire which was related economically to the Egyptian empire, but that is not certain. There is speculation that later Christian minorities fled the Nilotic areas to Darfur from the advent of Islam.[19]

The history of the Darfur area starts with three consecutive empires, the Taju, the Daju and the Keira/Fur, of which little is now know. Although there are few written sources about the successive empires or dynasties of the region, some can be found in travellers' guides. For example, the Arab traveller Al-Tunisi described the tribal relations of Darfur, and there were others too.[20] Early sources indicate that in the twelfth century the Daju people were the first to establish a strong empire in Darfur. These people believed themselves to be descended from the Nubian people, and therefore acted as the rulers of the area. After them, the Tunjur dynasty rose to power and it is certain that they spread the religion of Islam in the region. The Tunjurs ruled the area from the fourteenth to the sixteenth century, creating a vast empire that spread across the desert areas of the Darfurian territory.[21] In the seventeenth century, another dynasty came into play: the Keira clan of the Fur took over and established a dynasty that ruled for some time in the region. The Keira empire was established by Sulayman Solong (1596–1637) who took part in the religious transformation of the countryside.[22] The main enemy of the Keira was the Wadai Sultanate situated in eastern Chad. However, the empire conquered the city of el-Fasher, which by then became the capital of the country in 1791–92.[23] The Keira empire not only enlarged itself towards the western areas, but it went towards the east too. A very important economic and sociological step by the Keira empire was that it monopolised the slave business, and thus centralised the economic power in the area. The Keira empire was at its height in the eighteenth century and reached as far as Kordofan.[24]

The large empire had a completely new administrative system, which comprised four institutional divisions. One of them was south-west Darfur managed by the Fur people; the second was the south-eastern Darfur (Kidinger), and there were also divisions for north Darfur and east Darfur. By the end of the eighteenth century the empire was so huge that it even reached the Nile Valley.[25] The Sultanate was so vast and huge economically as well that it became the centre of the region: it controlled the silk, salt, copper, iron, livestock trades, and others, in the area. The slave trade was also important, as it brought payment in silk, glassware and horses from Egypt.[26] The Sultanate was thus the main centre of trade and military improvements for the African area, despite a short-lived Egyptian interlude that began in 1874–75 but was in turn defeated by the Mahdist movement in 1882.[27] After the end of the Mahdist state in 1898 the Sultanate was reinstated and the nomads were separated from the sedentary people.[28] The Sultanate however did not survive for long after this as an independent entity: during the First World War it was thought by the British that Darfur was falling under the influence of the Ottoman Empire and thus an expedition was launched to occupy the area.[29] After the occupation of the Darfurian sultanate, there was no conflict in the area for some time. The local leadership was formed by the so-called sultans, and they were called upon by the British to stabilise the area which had previously been a large kingdom in the western territories.[30] An important part of the British organisation for the future of the area was that by this distinction the black tribes and the nomad Arabic background tribes were more clearly differentiated, thus giving impetus to the later conflicts that grew roots exactly at this point in the history of the Darfur region.[31]

In the post-Second World War period most of the African states became independent as a result of the decolonisation programme. In 1956, Sudan also got its freedom, but Darfur remained an autonomous district inside the country. Thus, everything rather stayed the same, with the ethnic and cultural divisions that have existed from the beginning of the 1900s. The problem in Darfur originated in the British leaders' decision to concentrate power in the hands of a number of Khartoum university graduates, who were mostly Arabs, and they gained control of the area. When Gaffar Nimeiri came to power in Sudan, one of his decisions was to take away the autonomous status of Darfur in 1972, and he started to install his men into important positions.

Not only was Nimeiri's government a problem, but from the 1980s there were several droughts in the area which made it difficult for the nomads in the north to survive there, and it influenced a mass migration towards the south which further added to the problem that now exists.[32] With the conflict in Chad in the 80s and 90s, the weapons trade meant that arms started to flow into the area, intensifying the conflict which started at the beginning of the century. By 1989, Omar al-Bashir, a bloody dictator, had risen to power in Sudan, and he formed three provinces in Darfur: West Darfur (el-Geneina; also 'al-Junaynah' or 'El Geneina'), South Darfur (Nyala) and North Darfur (el-Fasher).[33] The indigenous population started to revolt against the government as the restrictions on them became harsher and harsher, thus came the 2003 incidents against the Khartoum government and the Janjaweeds.

A meat market in a refugee camp. (János Besenyő)

A market stall selling meat in el-Fasher. (János Besenyő)

Much of the civilian travel around Darfur is done in trucks like this one, carrying both goods and passengers. (János Besenyő)

2
AMIS I

One of the main problems concerning the Darfur area is that there is a common misunderstanding concerning the nature of the conflict between the Arabic Janjaweed and the mainly black African sedentary population in the region, and that the main reason for the conflict is a problem between Muslims and Christians. This is a misconception, since both the Janjaweed Arab forces and the sedentary black population are Muslims. In fact, there have been attacks on mosques by the Janjaweed during the course of the conflict.[1]

Again, other researchers find it convenient to conclude that the conflict is based on the numerous nationalities that swell in the area. It is true, however, that the Janjaweed militias are not of black ethnicity, but they are instead of Arabic descent. Nevertheless, the sedentary population is not Arabic, they have their own black African ethnic identity and they have different languages and cultural heritages from the Fur, the Masalit and the Zaghawa tribes which distinguish them from the Arabic-speaking Janjaweed who were recruited from small tribes from the north. The Arab Janjaweed are historically landless and that is one of the sources of the conflict that had erupted there.[2] However, there are also Arabic tribes that settled in the Darfur area which do not belong to either major ethnic group involved in the fighting, so the question has tended to be greatly simplified by researchers who are not familiar with all of the reasons for the conflict.[3] It is the opinion of one of the authors of this book, János Besenyő (who served in the region) that the real problem is that the government enabled the Janjaweed militias to commit raids with impunity against the sedentary non-Arab population. The Khartoum government's aggressiveness is the real underlying cause of the conflict that erupted between the sides in this region.

The Beginning of the Devastating Darfur Conflict

The problems began in 2003 when the Sudanese Liberation Movement (SLM) and its armed wing, the Sudanese Liberation Army (SLA), as well as the Justice and Equality Movement (JEM) – who represented some of the sedentary tribes of the Darfur area – took up arms against the government-backed Janjaweed forces, who committed 'ethnic cleansing' against the farming and agriculture-

A civilian truck attacked by insurgents in the al-Geneina area. (János Besenyő)

A Mi-24P or Mi-35P attack helicopter of the Sudanese Air Force, moving low over the bush. Gauging by its serial number 923 (applied in black on the boom) this example belonged to the first batch acquired by Sudan in the early 2000s. However, that helicopter is known to have been shot down on 17 July 2003, while this photograph was taken in autumn 2005. This leads to the conclusion that Khartoum acquired a replacement which was given the serial number of the lost example. (János Besenyő)

based population. The Khartoum-based forces hit back with full-fledged armies of Janjaweed mercenaries: they attacked dozens of villages, slaughtered civilians and raped women.[4] The attacks came to a halt on 3 September, but this was only temporary, and from 5 December the hostilities continued.[5] The fighting had a high death toll; 30,000 persons perished and the conflict created one million displaced people in the region. After various negotiations the government and the SLM reached an agreement and a ceasefire was concluded.[6] Nevertheless, the hostilities did not seem to cease and international bodies thought it could jeopardise the long-standing prospects for the peace accords. The breaking of the ceasefire continued and pillaging was ongoing, which threatened peace in the region and risked the escalation of the conflict. To aid the establishment of peace in the area even the Sudanese government, under the lead of Omar al-Bashir, tried to control the Janjaweed with varying degrees of success, mostly because of the lack of trust towards them.

Several international forces tried to intervene to protect the ceasefire; including the United States, which attempted to stabilise the situation. There were several reasons why this global power wanted to secure the protection of the Darfur area: among them was the Sudanese oil resources, the threat of religious radicals – which was always an important cause for the US – and the reduction of conflicts in the zone among Arabic and other rival ethnicities. The US acted with more than words, and they sent military experts to AMIS (African Union Mission in Sudan) and gave a huge amount of financial resources to the Sudanese government for the control of the disastrous situation.[7] When the US started to negotiate with the Sudanese government, it implied that the Janjaweed forces must be controlled, or that America would impose sanctions on the Bashir government's oil resources, which would severely hurt the Sudanese economy. Khartoum however never admitted fully the responsibility for the militias, but rather said that the conflict was the consequence of the Iraq war – or as they called it, occupation – a combined effect of the aggression against Muslims by the West. The dispute ended in good faith as the Sudanese government and the Western forces consisting of the UN, US and other powers reached an agreement on 16–18 July 2004 in Addis Ababa, and this was the beginning of the communication between Khartoum and the rebels.[8] This was not the final settlement, and on 23 August 2004 the talks continued in Abuja, where the AU (African Union) also took part as a coordinator in the peace-making effort, which finally achieved a relatively positive result between the warring sides, or at least the status quo for a beginning.[9]

The Creation of AMIS I

One of the most decisive peace agreements in the conflict was reached on 8 April 2004 between the sides under the supervision of several outside forces, including the US and the European Union. As a consequence, the need for an inclusive peacekeeping mission emerged from almost all of the sides, and the Sudanese government forces also finally consented to the dispatch of a peacekeeping operation to the area.[10] Following the preliminary measures of the AU, the final agreement on sending the troops to Sudan came on 28 May in Addis Abeba, when the basics of the peacekeeping mission of the AU were laid down.[11] This was the official beginning of the African Union Mission in Sudan as a peacekeeping operation, and was established by the aforementioned forces.

There were four steps carried out upon the establishment of the mission: a liaison office was established in Khartoum, the preliminary troop leadership and logistical tasks were carried out, the first military experts arrived at the scene and took responsibility for their tasks and finally observer groups were deployed to the conflict zone. At the start of the operation, almost 300 military observers were sent to the location of the conflict with the task of supervising the area.[12]

The headquarters of the peacekeeping mission was a group called the Ceasefire Commission which was newly inaugurated. The second in command was the vice president, Major General Festus Okonkwo, who arrived from Nigeria, and the lower levels

Officers of the Sudanese police, seen here with a utility vehicle in Darfur in September 2005. (János Besenyő)

Combatants of the SLA underway in Darfur in 2005. (János Besenyő)

President of Sudan Omar al-Bashir (sitting in the centre, with glasses and a cane) during a visit to AMIS in August 2005. (János Besenyő)

of leadership were dispatched from the European Union. Twelve persons formed the aforementioned commission, and all sides of the conflict were represented in it including the SLM and the Khartoum government.[13] The main intervention was conducted by this commission, and it was responsible for handling the most important affairs of AMIS.[14] The group was responsible for:

- controlling demining activities,
- monitoring the ceasefire,
- giving opinion on ceasefire violations,
- deciding on controversial measures,
- controlling the forces of the sides,
- managing the balance of power between the warring parties.

Under this leadership, these six areas of responsibility were introduced, and the peacekeeping officers started their work and to fulfil their mandate in the conflict zone. These officers were organised into observer groups, which concluded the task of monitoring ceasefire violations and the compliance with the ceasefire agreements.[15]

The chain of command worked quite well in AMIS: these groups reported to their Chief Military Observer, who reported to the commission, and thus the leadership was always able to understand the events on the ground first-hand. A lot of the officers were unarmed peacekeepers. These were mostly guarded by the African Union's forces because the government forces were not as reliable in this role.

In addition to the original 100–300 AU military experts the force decided to bring in more soldiers from Rwanda and Nigeria, which made the logistical situation more difficult to handle. Nevertheless, the US, the UN and European countries tried to help the AU with the logistical and financial crisis they were experiencing, however the African force did not like the Western organisations and countries meddling in their affairs, thus they decided that they would rather do it on their own without external assistance.

It was not only the military observers in need of protection and the civilian population also needed outside help because of the conflict. The AU – responding to these calls – created two or three battalions of soldiers, which would protect the civilians from the Janjaweed forces, but – according to Besenyő – these AU soldiers were brought together rather to exclude the Western forces from the area of operations. The European forces considered these battalions to have low standards of training and be unsuitable for the protection of a large civilian population like the one in Darfur, of almost one million people. Finally, the European and Western forces had to comply with the wishes of the AU because it was the main military power in the peacekeeping operation in Darfur while the Europeans only provided financial and logistical assistance.[16]

A problem with the deployment of the AU forces was that their members might be part of either one of the conflicting groups, thus – because all the parties claimed innocence – it was hard to establish who was responsible before troops could be dispatched to the location of an incident. Ceasefire violations also caused considerable work for the peacekeeping officers, thus it was hard to control the situation on the ground.[17] The civilians thus had to understand that what they previously expected – that the African forces would help them more because of their origins – did not actually happen in the end.[18]

According to Besenyő, the situation in the region was not very pleasant, since although the Sudanese forces were mostly kept under control, small scale attacks occurred in the conflict zone between the warring parties, which caused the security environment to degrade.

The arrival of the Rwandan Defence Force security platoon, carried by a Lockheed C-130 transport of the US Air Force (visible in the background), at el-Fasher Airport, in July 2005. (János Besenyő)

The arrival of the Nigerian police contingent in el-Fasher. (János Besenyő)

Soldiers of the Nigerian contingent of AMIS securing an area following another Janjaweed attack. (János Besenyő)

The largest problem was in the area where the civilian population was not defended well enough, and rapes and murder unfortunately accompanied the looting that occurred in Darfur even during the ceasefire.[19] According to Besenyő, the main problem was that the Arabic tribesmen were hurting the civilian black population in the area, and the atrocities committed by them were common, thus the government forces linked with the tribesmen of Arabic descent were seen to have a hand in the sufferings of the local black African sedentary population, who were trying to survive in a very difficult situation. The Sudanese government and the armed forces were not at all satisfied with the AU soldiers, who were considered to be foreigners, thus they tried to exclude them from the area, often handling face-to-face situations aggressively. The security of the peacekeeping officers was thus questioned and they were not at all protected in an area where fighting between the Janjaweed or the government forces and the rebels was regular. Because of the insecure conditions and the improper security environment, the situation of the peacekeepers was far from perfect, their activities thus were restricted, and their numeric inferiority made them prone to attacks.[20] The situation required a remodelling of the

Arrival of the Rwandan Defence Force contingent in el-Fasher of July 2005. (János Besenyő)

The AMIS camp outside Mournei, October 2005. (János Besenyő)

peacekeeping operation in October, but this did not help much with the dire security situation.

Since the mission had several weaknesses and its successfulness was brought into question, its potential disbandment was a continuous issue in the eyes of the appropriate leaders. Evacuation plans were drawn up for December 2004, but details were not fully described.[21] The arrangements for the mission were not at all comprehensive: there was insufficient drinking water, leave was not regulated, the logistics of the mission could not be called very thorough, since the chief officers according to some soldiers were rather indifferent to the fate of their officers on the ground, and they mainly stayed in the headquarters. The situation thus could be described as dire in the peacekeeper camps.[22]

Remodelling was not as successful as the leaders of the mission wanted, so the situation in the conflict zone escalated further. The AU could not avoid asking for help from the US and the European Union who sent consultants or experts to the area. The advisers from the European Union were mostly highly qualified participants but they did not fill ranks according to their qualification because the system was not well organised, and they had to resort to tasks that were below their training level. However, it happened several times that these officers were deprived of vital information and they were neglected by the AU because of organisational ineffectiveness in the peacekeeping operation's leadership.[23] Thus the status of these experts was not successfully established before 2006, so until then, the rank and task of the European military experts were not all the time clear.

The AMIS camp outside Malha, in August 2005. (János Besenyő)

3 AMIS II

AMIS I was not successful because of the insufficient number of its peacekeeping officers, and the AU did not send enough military observers to cover the whole area. The equipment was not good enough either, and the personnel of the mission was so small in number that it was impossible to fulfil their tasks properly. On 8 July 2004, the AU increased their peacekeepers to 80 persons, but this did not prove effective.[1] Because of the ineffectiveness of the mission, the AU – along with the UN – planned an expansion of the numbers deployed by September 2004. By 20 October 2004 the AU financial and military leadership approved a plan to expand the mission by 3,320 persons – including 2,341 soldiers, of which 450 were military observers.[2] This expansion was to be concluded for a one year term, and it was mandated for the following tasks: help the civilian population, checking compliance with the 8 April 2004 ceasefire agreement, helping refugees, maintaining a positive security environment in Darfur and trust-building activities. The expansion of the mission was to be carried out in five consecutive steps that were the following:

1. There was an initiative state, where the officers had to establish the new conditions for the expanded mission, designing the logistical and operational plans for the new operation. They wanted to expand, besides the logistical side, the campsites as well to be able to house the additional troops as expected. The leaders had to organise the dispatch of the new officers to their headquarters as well, and their logistical placement. Their final task was to acquire the necessary funds from external sources, since the AU was short on monetary funds for the expansion.
2. After that, a 30-day-long period followed, which created a conceptual start, when the facilities in the bases were significantly improved. The Ceasefire Commission was replaced by an organisation named Operation Command, which became the control body for the mission. It was based in el-Fasher, which was the centre of the Darfur conflict zone. Observer units were expanded, and their number was increased to 10 persons.

3. Fifteen days later the next step took place in the implementation of the mission-augmentation. At this time, emphasis was placed on the organisation of camps in the peacekeeping operation, and the Operation Command took over the military and administrative areas of the mission leadership. The number of peacekeeping officers was also raised, 60 of them were instructed in el-Fasher and they were dispatched to the conflict zone with the others soon after that.
4. Another 15 days after the settlement of the barracks and the training of new officers, a new frame of actions developed. One hundred and twenty more peacekeepers were sent to the newly created sites, which were expanded according to plans in this period. The security status of the soldiers was strengthened by new forces which arrived at the scene to help the unarmed officers in their duty and to protect them.
5. Seventy-five days after the starting point, new plans were devised. The building of new camps and the advancement of logistical and military improvements made it possible to await new peacekeeping officers to the conflict area. The soldiers and the accompanying security personnel kept coming, and their number increased by 120 officers.
6. Finally, 120 days after the initiation of the program 30 more peacekeepers were dispatched to the scene and this way the expansion of the military personnel was carried out.

These were, however, only plans, which were supposed to work, but unfortunately due to several reasons their fulfilment was not possible as envisaged. The number of the soldiers did not reach the desired level and the camps' logistical arrangements were not as effective as had been planned for. The number of peacekeepers did not reach the requested quantity due to mostly inappropriate conditions that made it difficult to organise the peacekeeping mission of the AU in an orderly way. All in all, by February 2005 the number of personnel in the mission had reached 1,446 persons, while the leadership of the peacekeepers awaited at least 4,000 people to participate in AMIS II as a proper aid to the ongoing operation. The AU Peace and Security Council however wanted to control the situation, thus it dispatched a committee to the area to assess the information available on the conflict zone so as to help to improve the situation according to the results of this inquiry.[3]

All of the preparations were officially finished by the leadership in November 2004. However, a new organisational structure was developed, as the Darfur Integrated Command took matters in hand, which was responsible for improving the situation on the ground. Logistical development was also an issue for the UN, US and the European Union, and so they created the Administration Control and Management Centre (ACMC).[4] After this, some administrative changes were concluded, for example the Khartoum office, which worked as a liaison organisation, was transferred to the AMIS Head of Mission, which took responsibility for the organisational capabilities, however the Ceasefire Commission and the CIVPOL (civilian police) contingent leadership were situated in el-Fasher and they controlled the military issues. The leadership of the Ceasefire Commission nevertheless remained the same, the Nigerian General Festus Okonkwo stayed in charge of the mission's

Troops of the Sudanese Defence Forces in Darfur, late summer 2005. (János Besenyő)

An Iveco 260 fuel tanker of AMIS. (János Besenyő)

operational management and the top police officer, Brigadier General Anand Pillay instructed the contingent, so there were some changes, whereas the leadership remained mostly the same.[5] Besides the logistical and organisational improvements, the communication area was not neglected either, as the officers in charge installed lots of new radios and high-tech equipment at the camps that connected the otherwise distant peacekeeping sectors to each other, and they even equipped military automobiles with appropriate apparatus to communicate properly among themselves.[6]

Notwithstanding the improvement of the AMIS mission, and the expansion of the operation into AMIS II, the logistical, organisational and communication innovations, the situation in the area remained dire. The Janjaweed and other insurgent organisations and armed bands did not stop harassing the innocent sedentary population in the conflict-torn territory, and the leadership of AMIS II seemed helpless to handle the situation. There were events that even made peacekeepers weary of the Darfur conflict and they felt empathy for the population of the Darfur region that had been constantly assaulted. There was an inccident which even raised the attention of Javier Solana, Secretary-General of the Western European Union: on 26 January 2005 Rahat Kabalong in Darfur was attacked by the Sudanese air force and approximately 100 people died in the incident which created apprehension among the peacekeepers.[7]

The peacekeeping operation was organised into sectors, which were mostly led by individual countries, though this aroused dissatisfaction among the leadership and the international community. That this was the way the things worked out in the peacekeeping camps of AMIS II and was due to the fact that there was no possibility of central control, because the distance between the sectors did not allow for a common leadership. Thus, control of the sectors was based in the areas that were prone to conflict. To understand better the geographic and logistic division of the camps, it is perhaps of importance to present the most important of them to the reader.

el-Fasher

The capital of Darfur was the headquarters for the AMIS II mission; nevertheless the environment in which the peacekeepers lived was not the most comfortable. The bare, partly desert area sometimes flooded with rainwater and the temperature rose as high as 50 °C. The weather is so unbearable that a significant number of the soldiers obtained apartments in the town thus avoiding the difficult circumstances the camp provided. Another problem was that the manpower should have been around 300 persons, but because of

AMIS camp outside Nertiti, seen in autumn 2005. (János Besenyő)

Rwandan troops constructing a sentry post outside the AMIS camp near Nertiti. (János Besenyő)

Rwandan troops leaving their camp for a patrol. (János Besenyő)

the transfer traffic, it often reached as high as 500 soldiers, which made the site overcrowded and the conditions for living in the camp difficult.

Nyala

The southern capital of Darfur is also far from ideally situated, but the circumstances are better than in el-Fasher. The security situation however was dire because many clashes occurred in the zone between the warring parties, with even AMIS II forces being attacked several times. The communication possibilities were nevertheless a lot better than in other places.

el-Geneina

In this area the weather was better than others, and since aid organisations worked on the site, life was not so unbearable in the territory. el-Geneina is the centre of West Darfur and the security environment in this zone was quite good compared to that of Nyala.

The AMIS camp outside Nyala, seen in November 2005. (János Besenyő)

A typical sandstorm about to hit the AMIS camp outside el-Fasher. (János Besenyő)

Kabkabiya

The Fur and Zaghawa tribes gather in this place and have formed a community in the elevated region. The area is so treacherous, that the Janjaweed forces did not dare to enter those parts, so the community of the tribes can live in relative peace there. However, the zone is not devoid of conflicts and exchanges of fire.[8]

Tine

This town is on the western side of Darfur, near Chad, and so there is much smuggling here. The biggest problem is the weather conditions, which make it very difficult for peacekeepers to work in the area. The place is largely desert and sandstorms are quite frequent, making it difficult to endure the given conditions.[9] The security situation however, was relatively normal, and there were few incidents that disturbed the ceasefire agreement.

Kutum

This relatively peaceful sector was headed by South Africans, and they controlled most of the events in the area.

Zalingei

This area was considered dangerous as many ceasefire violations occurred in the sector. The climate is rather mild so the place was, from that perspective, acceptable for peacekeeping officers to work in.

Al-Dein

The SLA had its headquarters situated in this area, thus it was inevitable that fighting occurred between the government forces and the SLA. Rebel forces also conflicted with each other on occasion, making the situation difficult to handle. The weather was somewhat harsh due to the windy conditions in the area.

The administrative units all had the following tasks:

- logistic administration, camp building, military observer group organisation in each headquarters
- communication with local leaders
- checking the security and supply of refugee camps
- controlling the movements of armed groups through patrols
- checking armed groups and preventing military escalation
- the maintenance of the warring parties, maintaining the ceasefire
- checking the security of military officers and observers
- disarmament measures taken by the officials
- performing humanitarian tasks

AMIS II was expanded, but there were several deficiencies that hindered the execution of the mission. The logistic organisation and the lack of finance caused several problems that made the implementation of the plans originally created by the heads of

Troops of the South African National Defence Force contingent at their outpost outside Kutum airfield in 2005. Next to the outpost is one of the omnipresent Toyota pick-ups, with a Casspir mine-resistant, ambush protected (MRAP) truck to the rear. (János Besenyő)

Mortar bombs collected by an explosive ordnance disposal team of the South African contingent with AMIS. (János Besenyő)

the mission much more difficult. The increment of the mission's capabilities did not help to better control the ongoing conflict between the Janjaweed and the SLA, so the mission did not fully achieve its previously expected goals. The committee that was sent to measure the activities of the mission arrived at a similar conclusion. The executive branch that was dispatched on 10 March 2005 was a composite group with representatives from the European Union, the US and the United Nations.[10]

Previously the committee also consulted with several members of the Sudanese leadership, including ministers and security chiefs, to facilitate their approach to the area and to mend enmities between the mentioned forces. Once they got the consent of the Khartoum cabinet, they started their work in the area. Naturally they visited the sites that were prone to conflict: these consisted of the military camps set up by the peacekeeper forces, and they evaluated what they saw there. The Ceasefire Commission was one of the main organisations with which the consultative board met and they discussed with the official leaders the situation on the ground. NGOs (non-government organisations) and other representative humanitarian forces were also monitored during the inspection, while refugee camps were examined too.

The result of the inquiry was mixed: the committee saw that the situation was rather difficult in the conflict zone. While it acknowledged the efforts of the AMIS II mission in consolidating the inspected areas, the members reacted to the dire state of the territory outside the control of the mission, where violations occurred

Specialists of the South African EOD team preparing a UB-32-57 pod still filled with 57mm S-5K unguided rockets – jettisoned by a fighter-bomber or attack helicopter of the Sudanese Air Force – for destruction. (János Besenyő)

every day and fighting between the two sides was common.[11] The delegation assessing the scenario concluded that the tensions had not diminished in the region despite the enormous efforts of the African Union's mission, and the number of displaced persons had now reached 1.4 million, with 200,000 refugees in Chad. The ethnic-tribal differences remained and the civilians were still in danger despite the efforts of the peacekeeping mission.[12] The situation at the refugee camps remained desperate, since the Janjaweed troops did not stop harassing the people living in the settlements designed to protect them. The government's mercenaries cruelly abused the civilian population and the displaced persons and consequently they were living in constant fear of the soldiers. The security forces were too weak and not trusted by the refugees and they did not have anybody to turn to. The pillaging thus continued and the government supported the Janjaweed and other militias.

Returning home was however not an option, because the Darfur region in which they previously lived was more dangerous than the area they now resided in. Darfur was also a harsh place, even worse than the refugee camps, because of the continuous ceasefire violations, rape and murder that fell upon the civilian sedentary population in the area. Even the aid organisations were helpless, since they were unable to intervene in the clashes that took place between the Janjaweed and the civilians. The report assessed that although the peacekeepers did a good job at maintaining the situation, they did not stop the conflict from escalating and the people lived in constant peril.

The Darfur Integrated Task Force (DITF) in Addis Ababa was perplexed with the conflict, as it did not have adequate resources to manage a proper response to the ongoing problematic issues: equipment and manpower were not sufficient, and they were in need of reinforcement if they wanted to improve the conditions of AMIS II on the ground.[13] The centre of the operations (in Darfur) was in no better condition either. The task force of peacekeepers worked in 18 camps and the number of the soldiers were not always sufficient relative to the size of the area and the tasks at hand. The mission had logistical problems: there were three components of the operation, a civilian, a military and a police contingent and they were sometimes at odds with each other, and their numbers were not appropriate at times to handle the difficult situations that could occur in the conflict-ridden area.

The preparation and education of the soldiers were at times not good enough, since some of them did not speak the languages important for a peacekeeper (generally English and/or French). This was a problem for the logistical organisation and the communication between the units.[14] The commission had several other problems with the AMIS II mission as well, as they missed the appropriate aid system in the Darfur conflict zone among the AMIS organisation. They objected also to the president of the Ceasefire Committee, since he was also the leader of AMIS II, which made it sometimes difficult to differentiate between leadership responsibilities. Regarding all these objections, the committee advised the African Union on some issues, but they did not seem keen to comply with the wishes of the executive board. The committee assessed as well that the peacekeeping mission tried to do its best to control the ethnic cleansing, however, they were not able to do so because the 2,259 persons who were at the scene proved to be insufficient to

Members of the commission monitoring the ceasefire seen with a Mi-8 helicopter chartered from Russia to support the work of AMIS. (János Besenyő)

A group of SLA fighters, armed with a miscellany of Soviet PKM machine guns, Belgian FN/FAL and Soviet-designed AK-47 or AKM assault rifles. (János Besenyő)

control the large land area and the roaming militias that devastated the conflict zone.

Despite the good intentions of the AMIS peacekeepers, the situation did not enable them to control the events which broke out during the conflict, and resulted in a decreasing belief in the soldiers' abilities to keep the peace in the area. The board had to report that – as mentioned before – the logistic, military and other capabilities of the peacekeeping operation lacked sufficient standards to be able to manage the issues that disturbed peace.[15]

The logistic organisational insufficiencies were obvious to the committee, as well as the lack of an adequate healthcare system that could support both the civilians and the military personnel. They also lacked the proper equipment and vehicles that could serve well in a peacekeeping mission such as AMIS II, and the transport possibilities were regarded as meagre by the investigation commission. They criticised as well that out of the 850 possible peacekeepers, only 170 soldiers were dispatched to the conflict zone and took active part in the peacekeeping tasks, including the protection of the refugees who were vulnerable and prone to the attacks of the Janjaweed militias. What they were delighted with was the participation of 20 female police officers in the peacekeeping operation and thus the gender issues of the mission were taken into consideration according to the

An officer of the South African police underway in the refugee camp outside Otash in November 2005. (János Besenyő)

committee.[16] After the delegation returned, the African Union took the ideas of the board into consideration, and as a result the African Union Peace and Security Council published a report regarding the situation of Darfur on 28 April 2005 which included the expansion of the military forces of AMIS to 7,731 people.[17]

After the committee's assessment, the representatives of Sudan, Nigeria, Eritrea, Chad, Gabon, Libya and Egypt met in Tripoli on 16–17 May 2005 to discuss the issue of Darfur. They concluded that Africans were able to handle the situation and they declared that they had to be the ones to solve the problems of the ongoing conflict, and so they stated that they wished to exclude the presence of other soldiers in the area.[18] There were voices of countries in the meeting who said that war crimes had been perpetrated in the Darfur conflict, but especially Sudan and Egypt protested against this accusation and requested a supervising committee to examine the country's situation, however the opposition forces in the conflict did not agree to this at all. Finally, in May 2005 AMIS II was completed and by June the mission expanded further to be able to solve the problematic issues in the Darfur conflict. The organisation, however conformed to its mandate by receiving the maximum 7,731 participants.[19]

4
AMIS III (AMIS II–E)

AMIS III was designed on the basics of the AMIS II mission, and it was created by the AU to extend the priorities and capabilities of the previous operation. It was established in order to enhance the logistical and military organisational preparedness of AMIS II, and this time safety was a major issue in the formation of the new peacekeeping organisation. The dispatch of several and various items of military equipment, such as helicopters and armoured vehicles, served as an important factor for improving the standards over the previous unit. The final number for AMIS III was declared by the AU as 6,171 personnel.[1] The details of the prepared mission were the following:

- AMIS III leadership organised Military Observer Groups (MOG) in the camps
- in every camp there had to be 2 MOGs
- 8 battalions in coordination with the existing sectors
- modification of camps in order to extend the territorial possibilities of the areas at hand

The structure of the new AMIS III was created as follows:

- the leading organisation was the Operation Command
- 8 sector bases
- 1 engineering unit

Rwandan troops preparing their weaponry before heading out for another patrol. (János Besenyő)

- military interpreters
- the Chadian Abeche Observer and Liaison Office with a 40-person-strong contingent
- 1 air mobility unit
- 1 security unit

AMIS III was created to be an enhancement of the AMIS II mission, and the organisers and planners of the new operation wanted to make sure that the freshly established peacekeeping force was able to overcome the problematic issues which AMIS II had faced before it. As before, the main issue was the dispatch of more soldiers, which was this time carried out partly by the EU Military Staff, which organised the deployment of several companies to the area of the conflict to strengthen the forces of the AU in Darfur.[2] The transportation issues regarding AMIS III were discussed between NATO, the EU and the US on 19 January in Eindhoven and further dispatch of military forces were agreed upon during the negotiations. An airlift mission was organised by NATO and the EU based on the experience of the previous commitments and a Joint Forward-Based Movement Cell was established.[3] Notwithstanding the good intentions of AMIS III, the problematic issues remained the same and the difficulties had not really been solved by the new mission's activities.[4] The same deficiencies emerged as before, as the logistical and military organisation of the mission was incomplete, the language knowledge of the military officers lacked the proper level and the Khartoum government were still at odds sometimes with the mission's leadership as they did not like competition in their country. To describe the situation it is perhaps worth citing an entry from Besenyő's personal log who was a peacekeeper with the AMIS mission at the time:

> After coming back from the holidays I started to work again, but during the last two weeks the situation has deteriorated to a level that I could move out of the Headquarters only with an armed escort. In spite of this, I spent a significant part of my week in the camps and in the operational area. The current security status is very unstable and unpredictable because both the government forces and the insurgents keep attacking each other as well as their real or perceived opponents. And mostly we are these opponents… In sector 5, SLA militants captured a patrol of ours and took all their equipment (cars, radios, etc.) except their clothes, so the patrols were forced to return to camp on foot, walking several kilometres on bare feet without boots. In the same sector, the Senegalese soldiers went on a "strike" and refused to perform any work until the AU had paid off their arrears of salary. As the weapon is in the hands of soldiers and they possess the tacit support of their officers, the mission leaders seek quick agreement. The recent strike of interpreters (about 40 people) took more than two weeks before the AU was ready to allocate a portion of the several months' worth unpaid wages to them. The Senegalese also claimed that the security situation has deteriorated to such an extent that even the normally paid personnel are reluctant to tread into the field, let alone those unpaid.
>
> Meanwhile, members of the Sudanese army attacked a refugee camp near Nyala, where several people, including Sudanese soldiers also, lost their lives or got injured. The soldiers kidnapped one of the leaders of the refugee camp inhabitants, resulting in a spontaneous attack on the Sudanese police and soldiers by the inmates. The situation in the camp is still rather tense; AMIS patrols are trying to patrol the area more frequently. Unfortunately, we received several reports about clashes in the other sectors as well.
>
> The Canadians, while I was on leave, sent 5,000 maps for the mission, as the patrols were unable to effectively patrol and did not know the area well. On one occasion a patrol did not actually find the village it had been sent to. Now we have updated maps, the distribution of which is still in progress. However, out of the 105 armoured vehicles – offered by the Canadians – only 35 were allowed by the Sudanese government (these have already arrived in Dakar) to be brought into Darfur. The AU leaders claimed that either all arrived or none of them. At present it seems that the Sudanese prefer the second version. This is confirmed by the fact that this evening the Sudanese government armed forces held a parade around the camp again, though not with as significant forces as they did in the beginning of the month (three large trucks, seven small cars equipped with machine guns and 200–250 soldiers equipped with small arms). We have followed the parade in front of the JLOC building with our African colleagues. One African officer was in an almost complete shock when he saw the Sudanese soldiers celebrating and shooting. A European military adviser laconically asked him if he had a bellyache as his face was like if he had bitten on a lemon. Though right after he cut back on humour, both he and the others seemed quite frightened by the parade. I tried not to show it, but my stomach clenched as I recalled that in the camp of almost 700 people, only the Gambian company, the Kenyan military police and the South African demolition experts had weapons. It meant approximately 150 people. If the Sudanese really tried to attack the camp, we would not really be able to defend ourselves. Luckily, apart from the scaring, they did not want anything else.
>
> Behind the scenes, the negotiations between the AU and the UN continued on the subject that the World Organisation would take over the leadership of this mission from the Africans, similarly to the mission of the Nuba Mountains. Its date was scheduled to be on April 1, 2006. Probably that is why – unlike their former stance – the Africans want the EU, the US and the Canadian experts (JLOC) to stay at least until the end of March. According to the United Nations local Danish military liaison, the UN would only take the operational command, the communications and logistics (as they were unable to function!), while the African countries would provide the leadership of teams.[5]

Troops of the Senegalese contingent of AMIS in front of one of the Mil Mi-8 helicopters deployed to Sudan in support of the peacekeeping mission. (János Besenyő)

A patrol car struck in a stream in the Mukjar area. (János Besenyő)

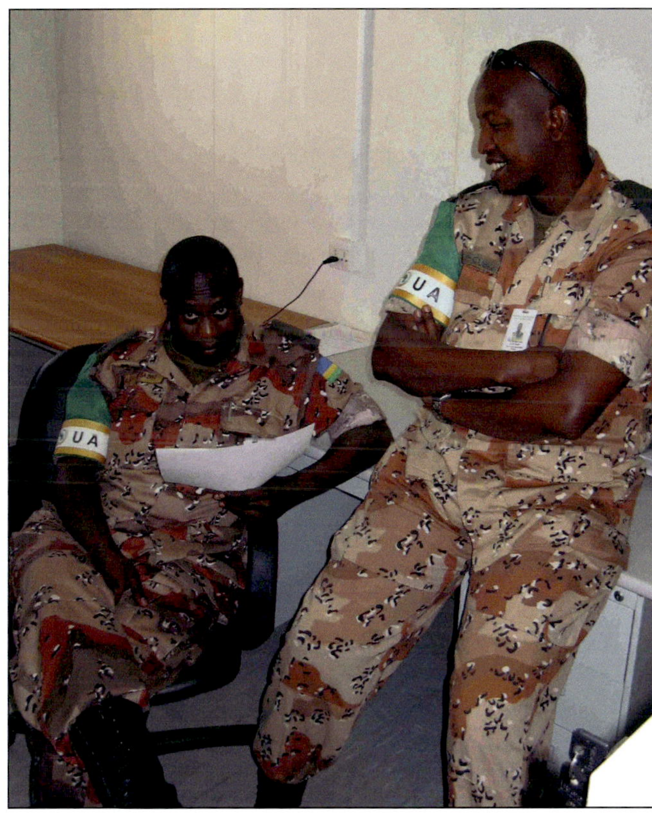

Officers of the Rwandan Defence Force contingent of AMIS in JLOC office of the AMIS camp outside el-Fashir, in 2005. (János Besenyő)

The mission could have been a success, but instead the AU was struggling with a bunch of financial and logistical problems, this way the AMIS III organisation could not totally fulfil the expectations as an extension of the AMIS II mission, because the same operational deficiencies remained at large. Since the issues had not been solved and the placement of military officers was incomplete, the inflow of peacekeepers was halted by September 2005, and they were dispatched to the conflict zone late. As mentioned previously, the logistical problems had a great effect on the mission, sometimes there was not enough water, the accommodation was not organised well, and the sanitation was not always on a bearable level at the camps.[6] Besides the logistical problems, at least some good news appeared: 647 vehicles arrived at the scene and armoured personnel carriers were dispatched with them as well, so the military contingent of AMIS III was seriously strengthened in terms of military force on the ground. The AU also tried to help the mission through the participation of NATO in training the peacekeepers to reach the level that was required for the operation.[7]

However, despite the efforts of AMIS III, the situation deteriorated further and an incident occurred in the territory which showed that the area was still prone to conflict. On 8 October 2005, a military contingent was attacked in Khor Abechi and six military observers died. The cruel assault had an immediate effect: a committee was set up to inquire about the assault which cost the lives of the peacekeepers. The board came to a conclusion that there were three causes for the terrible event:

A sentry outside the Khor Abechi camp. (János Besenyő)

- the AMIS III mission was underequipped and the military contingent was not strong enough or prepared enough to counter these type of attacks.
- armed response was missing due to misunderstandings from the peacekeeping officers.
- the mission lacked the capabilities to assess information preventing the attack from taking place.[8]

There were other difficulties in the mission as well. For example, the Sudanese forces hindered the activity of AMIS III wherever it could because they regarded the mission as an intrusion into the affairs of the Sudanese government.[9] The conflict between the government and the AMIS forces was so unmanageable that the two sides finally met on 27 August 2005 to discuss the problematic issues at hand and to come to an agreement. The negotiations were held over the following issues:

- weapon usage of AU officers
- participation of NATO troops
- participation of US soldiers
- AMIS III assistants and soldiers
- the rules of mission conduct
- the increment of AMIS III
- airport management
- common understanding between AMIS and the Khartoum government
- compliance with UN Resolution 1593

As a result of the meeting, AMIS and the Sudanese forces agreed that they would not interfere in each other's businesses, and the Sudanese would not intrude into the affairs of the AMIS III mission. Nevertheless, the pending issues did not changed and the situation of the peacekeepers, which remained the same on the ground.

In the meantime, the AU Security and Peace Council extended the mandate of the AMIS III mission on 20 October 2005.[10] At that time, there were some amendments they wanted to implement concerning the mission. The main issue was concentrated around the number of soldiers, which they still found insufficient for the appropriate handling of the conflict situation. Eventually they decided to expand the personnel of the AMIS III operation by 4,000 soldiers, which would amount altogether to 12,300 peacekeepers. The raising of the number of the peacekeepers would have seriously helped the mission in implementing its provisions and plans regarding the peace-making process, however many military observers never arrived at the scene due to organisational, administrative and logistic problems. The number of soldiers was however expanded and thus the peacekeeping operation boosted its effectiveness thanks to the new organisational arrangements. Even humanitarian aid had been revived and its organisations tried to make efforts to solve the situation of the refugees who suffered at the hand of the Janjaweed and other militias.

The situation regarding the Darfur conflict however remained the same, as the government-affiliated forces loomed in the area. The AMIS III peacekeepers had a hard time as well, because the Khartoum regime resorted to tactics of sometimes revoking the visa rights of the soldiers and even restricting airport access for them.[11] On occasion the Sudanese militias painted their vehicles to look like UN cars, thus a confusing situation appeared: the SLA apparently then attacked peacekeepers because they thought that the Janjaweed who assaulted them while using the painted cars were AMIS personnel. Nevertheless, the SLM rebels did commit criminal acts against AMIS from August 2005 and the peacekeepers were helpless against them.[12]

Partly because of the inefficiency of the peacekeepers to maintain the security state of the conflict zone, both the rebel groups as well as the Sudanese forces criticised the relevance of the peacekeeping operation as it was not able in their eyes to control the conflict zone with appropriate measures. The Darfur conflict however remained as complex as ever, since not only did the humanitarian situation deteriorate, but from neighbouring Chad a significant number of soldiers arrived due to the complicated issues in that country, and these forces joined the rebel groups. Thus, fighting occurred between several factions in the conflict which made it more difficult to come to an understanding for the opposing sides.

The people who were forced to refugee camps now amounted to 1.8 million persons, which is a huge number, and it reflected upon the humanitarian situation of the country. Despite the huge amount of financial support the mission received after 26–27 May 2005 – $312 million – a significant decrease in funds was expected by 2006.[13] The organisational and logistic difficulties were sometimes difficult to handle, for example, the accommodation of some of the peacekeepers was not always appropriate for the AU personnel, the relationships and diplomatic communication channels were not perfectly created. Because of several reasons – and due to financial deficiencies – the AU wanted to find partners to develop relations in the peacekeeping arena, thus it started to cooperate with the UN and other organisations more intensively. The new committee that was dispatched to Darfur assessed the opportunities regarding the mission and concluded:

1. Organisational tasks:
    - the development of the Ceasefire Commission
    - better planning execution
    - communicational and informational upgrade of the previous situation
    - unification of the leadership structure
    - improvement of the living conditions and the training of the peacekeepers
    - improvement of legal cases
2. Military tasks:[14]
    - The most important task was the addition of appropriate numbers of soldiers to the AMIS III mission, but in the meantime, several other problems were at hand:
        a. the eighth battalion of the military contingent was to be added
        b. organisational problems were clarified regarding the military observers' proper tasks
        c. transportation and aviation issues were suggested to be developed
    - Operational capacity-building:
        a. nocturnal missions were to be organised better
        b. the improvement of reconnaissance capabilities was advised
        c. language problems (Arabic and English knowledge) had to be handled
    - the daily reports on the operational results were not always appropriate
    - the operational issues were not always adequately handled

4. Police capabilities:[15]
    - EU and UN experts were sent in order to help the officers at the scene with their tasks and gave advice to them.
    - the refugee situation improved since the Sudanese forces worked together with the AMIS III peacekeepers, and they cooperated so well, that the humanitarian issues were easier to solve
    - because of language difficulties the police corps were sometimes incomplete
    - the police cared more about the civilians who suffered from the consequences of the conflict

5. Logistic cases:[16]
    - a so-called Joint Logistic Operations Command was to be created to ameliorate the circumstances of the operation and to improve the logistical deficiencies that were created in the AMIS III
    - with the establishment of a hospital in el-Fasher the healthcare opportunities and facilities have been expanded, and the opportunities regarding healthcare became better
    - technical equipment and communication possibilities were found weak and had to be mended

Because of these facts issued in the reports, and since the mission suffered from several weaknesses and the new version, AMIS III, did not bring any actual practical changes in efficiency to resolve the conflict, the experts suggested a change or at least turning to other organisations for help, mainly the UN.[17]

Ultimately, the problem with AMIS III was that despite the numerous efforts that the AU peacekeeping mission made to improve the conditions of the conflict, there was no real result and the civilian population of Darfur continued to be harassed. Salim Ahmed Salim – who was the leader of the negotiations – expressed his satisfaction with the AU's participation in the Darfur issue,[18] and he stated that the results of the operation were more than what was previously expected from them. He also was of the opinion that the conflict could only be solved by Africans and that they should be in charge of the operation. He emphasised the importance of the other organisations as well, but he insisted that the leadership should be in the hands of Africans, and that Europeans should take advice from them about the conflict.

The complex and unresolved status of the Darfur conflict led to the assessment of the people in charge that a change was due to happen to the AMIS III mission, and on 10 March 2006 when the AU Peace and Security Council held its session, they decided to turn to the United Nations to take over the operation.[19] The decisions they made however were not always clear to the participants: some of the important details on how the changeover to the UN should be executed were not appropriately designed. There were various logistical and organisational deficiencies that hindered the transition of the organisation to the UN and the priority was to pass over the operation and not care about it further. The problem was that African leaders were still of the opinion that the mission should rely mostly on Africans and they did not have a proper logistic order by which this change would take place. Because of the Africans' exclusion of the Europeans from the main information flow they would not receive the relevant instructions on how to conduct the transfer of the mission from the AU to the UN. Although for further clarification of implementation of the plan the Europeans sent a delegation to Addis Ababa on 15–17 May 2006, the Africans did not truly rely on their opinions.[20] In order to restore good communications between the sides, the Europeans went once more to Addis Ababa on 23–24 May 2006, and it soon came to light that the AU transition requirements were not feasible in the way they imagined it. Even so, the logistical organisation was not appropriate, which made the arrangements more difficult to complete. The organisational requirement of contractor Pacific Architects and Engineers (PAE) took roughly 126 days.[21]

The statistic requirement and the logistical organisation would have taken a lot of effort from AMIS, but the head of the Mission Operations Command did not plan the transitions of AMIS III according to the required measures, instead they wanted to make changes according to their leaders' opinion, thus the formal issues were not taken seriously enough.

A patrol from the Nigerian Army mounted on a Toyota 'technical'. (János Besenyő)

The logistical and organisational planning of the mission was difficult to execute, thus the AU wanted to rely on international help and aid to complete its goals. The UN and others were lacking the relevant forces and financial resources to comply with the wishes of the AU. Finally, after several negotiations AMIS agreed to solve the problems in time.[22]

NATO become impatient, because they insisted on the transition of the mission, and they implied that they would participate instead of the UN in the operation if they did not.[23] This conclusion did not win the appreciation of the AU and the Khartoum regime, thus the Sudanese government turned to another solution, they wanted to take things into their hands, thus preserving for themselves the right to direct the operation and excluding the unwanted international forces from the mission arena.

There was a constant difficulty in the mission as the rebel groups and other participants in the conflict were unpredictable, and they began to intermingle and the handling of the situation became more and more complex. The main problem was that the rebels did not think that they would achieve results in this kind of environment and thought that the negotiations in the long term would bring them insecurity. The rebels were divided into several smaller groups which had different aims and goals to achieve, and finally the AU could not handle the situation any further and the smallest groups were excluded from the peace talks.

The other issue at hand was the border area between Chad and Sudan which was considered Sudanese territory by the Khartoum regime, and they stated to the European negotiators that they were not willing to give up the area to the Chadian government because that would affect their country's sovereignty. Ali Osman Taha, the vice president of Sudan also acknowledged to their counterparts that the issue of the UN takeover was not supported by the Sudanese government. The other partner in the talks, Alpha Oumar Konaré took a middle position by saying that he neither supported nor resisted the mission, but more likely the AU had doubts about a mission taking place under the supervision of the UN.[24] The problem was that the rebels started to doubt the AU because for the above mentioned reasons people thought that the Sudanese leaders were close to the AU and they would decide against the sedentary people and the SLM who would have much to lose from this cooperation.

The SLM and the other oppressed organisations thus wanted the help of the UN and the European organisations, but they had had enough of the ineffective dialogues between the warring sides so they did not want to take responsibility for the issue. In addition, the financial situation was difficult to handle, which thus hindered the process even as the conflict continued to be severe and there seemed to be no solution.

On 15 May 2006, the AU Peace and Security Council met and discussed the issue and reached a result that despite the Abuja negotiations and the participation of various African leaders in the talks supplemented by the US, EU, Great Britain and Canada, were at a stalemate and no real progress could be presented. The result was that the only parties included in the eventual declaration were the Sudanese government and the SLM Minawi group; the JEM for example, refused to agree to the negotiations.[25] The Darfur conflict however, despite the agreement, had not been solved and

A group of SLA combatants armed with PKMs, AK-47/AKMs and RPG-7 rocket propelled grenades in a typical Toyota pick up, used for transportation by all the parties involved in this conflict. (János Besenyő)

the transitional issues remained difficult, so there were a lot of issues that still had to be solved for the successful transition.

Nevertheless, the problematic issues continued and the fighting was ongoing notwithstanding the agreement. The attackers did not spare anybody, AMIS III and even police stations were targets for the fighters and a policeman died in one assault.[26] There was also a terrible incident in Camp Misteria, where a Nigerian officer died and several others were injured when the camp was attacked with RPGs and assaulted.[27] Chad also became involved in the conflict, since the Zaghawa tribe and Chadian rebels fought together against the civilians at the border, which complicated matters. AMIS III itself suffered from other troubles as well, for financial issues and healthcare problems were not handled according to requirements.[28]

All things considered, the vice Secretary-General of the mission, Hédi Annabi, on 4 April 2006 tried to assess and explain the situation to the UN Secretary Council. His data included the facts that the conflict was ongoing and the conditions were dire. He expressed his negative thoughts on the Abuja negotiations as well. He then summarised his ideas regarding the mission:

- expansion of AMIS
- developing better AU-UN communications
- the transition of AMIS III to the UN

The difficulties around the creation of the new UN mission arose fast and the existing difficulties continued to be present. However, AMIS III was in favour of transferring the mission to the UN and complied with the wishes of the international community. The Western governments, such as Great Britain and the US, were eager to persuade the Khartoum government to concede to the conditions given by the global community. The Eastern countries, like China and Russia, gave way to their concerns about the rights of the Sudanese leaders in the implementation and transfer of the mission. The African organisation of course supported the African way of resolving the problems.[29]

The mission was functioning, but the international groups supporting AMIS III wanted to improve the operation, so they tried to persuade the AU to expand the capacity of the mission. Thus, on 12 May 2006 the Forward Joint Mission Headquarters was established, which would have two subdivisions called the Joint Logistic Staff and the Joint Operations Staff.

The new positions were to be filled mostly from the people already in the mission, but at the beginning of June, the AU also asked for six experts from the partner organisations. The EU proposed to fill four of the six positions, which were promised to be resolved as of 26 June 2006.[30] However, it was promised that the new headquarters would be established by 2007, but it was not executed properly in reality. Ultimately, no joint operations centre was established for the UN-AU mission.[31] The above mentioned organisations advised the AU to be careful in the training of the officers they dispatched and ensure they were prepared for the mission so they did not cause problems as on the previous occasions.[32] In spite of the warnings, nothing changed and the AU again caused several problems for its fellow institutions, notwithstanding that from 29 May a UN expert also assisted the AU in implementing the required reforms.[33]

Another sandstorm approaching the AMIS camp outside el-Fasher. (János Besenyő)

The AMIS camp outside Shangil Tobaya, seen in November 2005. (János Besenyő)

An aerial view of the AMIS camp outside Um Barro, in 2005. (János Besenyő)

The next stage of the inquiries was an investigative delegation dispatched by the UN to the conflict zone between 4–10 June 2006.[34] The delegation went to Darfur, met with many leaders in the country, and they put together a complex report that characterised the situation in the area. They met with Omar al-Bashir, with whom they tried to cooperate and find a common solution to the mandate of the future United Nations-African Union Mission in Darfur (UNAMID); however, the Sudanese president opposed the idea of full-fledged authority for the organisation because he argued that it would hurt the Sudanese army and militias on the ground. AMIS was just right for them because of its feebleness and inability to interfere with the Khartoum government.

Their answer was negative to the creation of UNAMID, since they did not want a stronger UN force to take matters into their hands.[35] The delegation's opinion clearly advocated the creation of the UNAMID force, and the AU leader Konaré was also in favour of AMIS III and the establishment of the AU-UN-led future organisation as well. He was aware of the fact that the AU had financial difficulties in assisting with the creation of a peacekeeping operation. The other measure Konaré wanted to improve was the number of the peacekeepers serving in the mission, which he wanted to raise to 10,000, which – in his opinion – would be enough to better control the Darfur conflict. The delegation approved of Konaré's opinion since they considered the situation in the conflict zone as quite devastating and that serious help was needed for the AU if the situation was to be improved.[36] The African leader then came up with yet another idea, that he would meet with heads of states related to the mission and the conflict to discuss the opportunities in the future AU-UN cooperation. The delegation was supportive of the idea, but they found that the AU was lacking the proper logistics for such an effort. Their advice was to add between five and eight battalions to the contingent so the African force would be more able to execute its tasks. Nevertheless, they were doubtful of the Africans' capabilities.

In continuation of the transition process, in November 2006 the UN and the AU started a negotiation which led to a three-step draft to secure the ongoing changes. First, a logistical supplementation would take place with the help of the World Trade Organization, then the UN was willing to give 2,250 officers to boost the number of peacekeepers in the mission, and finally, they planned to assume control over the whole mission.[37] The plan at first concerned only logistic leadership, not the military tasks. The transition period between 2006 and 2007 was difficult, but by 2007, some observers were sent by the UN to AMIS III.

The process progressed further, and by 28–29 January 2007, a negotiation took place between the UN and the Africans to prolong the transition in three phases. Firstly, the UN sent 105 experts to the mission, then military, police and civilian contingents were deployed as follows:

- 2,250 military personnel
- 301 police experts
- 295 civilian humanitarian workers

For the third phase, the implementation of a joint UN-AU force of 17,300 military officers and 3,300 policemen was planned. General Anyidoho (the DITF leader) was the representative officer for the execution of the draft. The AMIS representative was Brigadier General Ephraim Rurangwa, and both of them carried out their tasks appropriately, although the Khartoum regime slowed down the transition process.[38] Meanwhile, several events occurred on the ground and in February 2007 the talks restarted between the sides. The problem was that new violence erupted in the conflict zone and not only participant soldiers, but AMIS military personnel were attacked as well.[39]

The next important step was a negotiation that took place in New York on 7 March 2007, when all the parties (the UN, US, EU, AU and other participants) gathered around. The following results were reached at the table:

- a joint UN-AU intermediary council is to be set up
- development of humanitarian and security issues at the conflict zone
- the political and peacekeeping solution of the conflict

- talks to be held between the UN-AU to find a solution to the difficulties raised by the Sudanese government
- compliance with the ceasefire agreement
- get the JEM join the negotiations
- to give a role to Eritrea in the Darfur conflict

Other results were achieved as well: the number of soldiers was raised to 19,000 military officers and 3,700 policemen and the participants agreed upon the need for persuading Omar al-Bashir to agree to the operation. The financial aid was to be given by the financers, and until June 2008 the UN could join in.[40]

The biggest problem with the operation of AMIS III was that the AU's financial capabilities were weak, and the partners drew the conclusion that without help the mission would fall apart. After tiring negotiations and the reluctance of the AU to let go of their ideas, they finally agreed to continue the talks on 28 March. By this time, the AU realised that the 'African way' did not work perfectly and they were more cooperative than before. Following the meetings, on 5 April the representatives of the AU and the UN held talks to agree on the establishment of the hybrid AU-UN mission situated at the current locations of AMIS III. From the 105 experts, 59 officers were dispatched, the second part would be carried out in August 2007, and the entire transition of the mission into a hybrid operation would happen in the middle of 2008.[41]

Following the movement of the negotiating parties, on 16–17 April in New York the faster implementation of the new UN-AU hybrid force was advised, and surprisingly the Khartoum regime accepted the modifications.[42] The transfer was promoted even by Bashir himself who advised the acceleration of the process.[43] Since the AU had lost several men during the fighting, their trustworthiness came into question in the eyes of the partners, who met on 20 April to discuss the issue, with the following results:

- the US helped in improving seven camps in 184 days from the dispatch of the soldiers
- the donors requested that the US build containers for the housing of the soldiers
- the EU contributed 45 million Euros to the mission funds
- joint financial support was agreed upon by the donors

The financial aid was $16 million, which was a considerable amount considering that it was for the setting up of two new battalions, and reports said that more was needed.[44] Finally, after high level negotiations took place, on 23 May a joint resume was reported by the AU and the UN to the office of the Secretary-General of the UNSC (United Nations Security Council), and the partial transition of AMIS III to the UN forces became official.[45] After this step, the UNSC issued Resolution S/2007/468, and thus the official creation of the UNAMID hybrid UN-AU force came into effect. According to the new numbers, 19,555 soldiers would participate in the future operation, and the basis for the mission was to be laid down by October 2007. As the decision was accepted by the parties, the AU became inactive and as a NATO investigative group observed, they wanted the UN to do the work in the transition process.[46] Because of this, the attackers targeted AMIS personnel as well and on 7 April 2007, a high ranking soldier was assaulted.[47] The UN soldiers were also targeted sometimes by the indigenous forces and, for example, on May 25 some military officers were assaulted and an Egyptian soldier died.[48] Other problems occurred on the ground as well; AMIS personnel refused to allow UN soldiers to enter Camp Tawila in June 2007. The Africans and the UN sorted things out but this was one of the incidents which showed the animosity that surrounded the conflict zone.[49] By the end of 2007, the UN-AU hybrid force's leadership, consisting of Special Representative Rodolphe Adada and the mission commander, the Nigerian Major General Martin Luther Agwai, started the preparations of the operation.[50] Continuing the negotiations the UN and the AU agreed on trying to move forward according to the 'African model', so the African orientation of the mission was not interrupted regardless of the hybrid nature. Nevertheless, European soldiers were out of the question according to the AU and the Sudanese.[51]

The operations – by June 2007 – received the following supplies:[52]

- 2 technical units
- 1 military hospital (level III)
- 1 military hospital (level II)
- 1 transport unit
- 1 communication unit
- 1 engineering unit
- 1 logistics unit
- 1 transport helicopter unit
- 1 aerial reconnaissance unit
- 1 combat helicopter unit
- altogether, the support consisted of 2,250 persons

The budget of AMIS III was so low, that it was obvious at that time that the operation could not survive without the help of the UN and 2008 would signal the start of the hybrid formation of the mission.[53]

After important documents were created on 12–13 July 2007 defining the new operation,[54] the name UNAMID (United Nations-African Union Mission in Darfur) was jointly accepted by the parties. The negotiations were continued on 15–16 July in Tripoli and Darfur and the AU and UN delegates talked about the developments regarding the Darfur situation. The UN-promised increase in the number of the soldiers was only partially successful, as the partners only gave 2,250 soldiers for the new mission. The preparations, however, were ongoing and by August, the logistics of the operation were improved.

AMIS was not efficient at the time, since it remained inactive because of the rainy weather and security reasons, and it executed only one third of its usual patrols.[55] Even the AMIS leadership was aware of the fact that the mission was falling apart, and they needed the aid money to keep on working. A lieutenant colonel described the situation as difficult and he was certain that the raising of the number of the contingent would not help much with the improvement of the mission, and his opinion was that the failure of the training and equipment of the African officers was a main factor in the decline of the mission. The rebels and the government militias were both at fault for obstructing the peacekeepers' work. Thus, the African soldiers and the mission commander thwarted the work of the mission.[56]

The Establishment of the UNAMID Force

The creation document for UNAMID was published on 31 July 2007 by the UNSC (Resolution 1769).[57] After the establishment of the organisation, the UN wanted to know which partners would give additional resources to the mission on 1–3 August 2007, and they requested from them:

- 8 infantry battalions
- 3 reconnaissance companies

The omnipresent and highly-popular Toyota Land Cruiser – frequently acquired via the United Arab Emirates – was the primary utility vehicle of virtually all the parties involved in the Darfur War. The example to the left is shown in a camouflage pattern applied on dozens of Land Cruisers operated by the Janjaweed (reorganised as the Rapid Support Forces/RSF in 2013). Most of these were converted into 'technicals' through the addition of pintle-mounted machine guns – in this case a 12.7mm DShK of Soviet/Russian origin. The example to the right is shown in the typical peacekeeping 'white overall' of the AMIS contingent, and with long benches for a total of eight troops in the cargo area, as used by Nigerian and Rwandan contingents in 2004–2006. (Artworks by David Bocquelet)

The Rwandan Defence Force was one of the first export customers for Land Systems OMC RG-31 Nyala MRAPs of South African origin, 76 of which had been acquired in 1996 and deployed intensively during the First and Second Congo Wars (fought 1995–1996 and 1998–2003, respectively). Based on the design of the Mamba armoured personnel carrier (which utilised the chassis of a Toyota Dyna 4x2 truck), the Nyala utilised the chassis of a Unimog truck. Its armour protected the crew of two – and up to six passengers – from bullets of up to 7.62mm calibre, while a V-shaped all-steel welded monocoque hull protected the occupants from a blast equivalent to two Soviet-made TM-57 anti-tank mines detonating simultaneously. While the Rwandans serving with AMIS tended to install 12.7mm DShK heavy machine guns, as shown in the left artwork, contingents assigned to UNAMID tended to use lighter 7.62mm M60s. (Artwork by David Bocquelet)

Designed in the late 1970s and introduced to service in the 1980s for the South African police and armed forces, the Casspir was one of the first MRAPs manufactured in large numbers. The Casspir had the capacity to carry a crew of two and up to 12 fully armed passengers in an armoured steel body (the bottom of which was V-shaped and proven to protect the occupants from the heaviest anti-tank mines). It gained fame during the so-called 'bush war' or 'border war' in Angola and South West Africa/Namibia in the 1980s, where a wide range of automatic weapons were often mounted singly or in pairs above the forward crew compartment. Hundreds of Casspirs were exported in the 1990s and 2000s, and several contingents serving with AMIS and later UNAMID utilised them in Darfur. The first of these were the South Africans, who brought with them about a dozen – apparently – unarmed vehicles. Painted in white overall, these tended to carry black title 'AMIS' under the driver's cab in 2005: this was subsequently replaced with a larger black title 'UNAMID'. (Artwork by David Bocquelet)

Amid rising tensions and several attacks on AMIS troops, in June 2005 the government of Sudan agreed to the deployment of 105 armoured personnel carriers on loan from Canada. These comprised 100 AVGP LAV I Grizzly armoured fighting vehicles (based on the Swiss MOWAG Piranha I) with a 12.7mm heavy machine gun and a 7.62mm machine gun in a Cadillac-Gage turret, and five Husky armoured recovery vehicles. Delivered via Senegal starting from 17 November 2005, the Grizzlies were operated by the Nigerian and Senegalese contingents, amongst others, but maintained by civilian contractors. (Artwork by David Bocquelet)

Proving too small and ill-equipped to counter the Janjaweed campaign, in 2008 AMIS was reinforced by a UN peacekeeping contingent designated UNAMID. Swelling to more than 22,000 strong, this eventually managed to curtail Janjaweed activity in Darfur, but only with a more robust mandate, much greater troop presence, and supported by additional heavy equipment. By 2010, UNAMID included the 812-strong Task Force 980: a battalion of the Royal Thai Army, including combat engineers, infantry, armour, and support elements, with equipment including – amongst others – Cadillac-Gage LAV-150 armoured personnel carriers. (Artwork by David Bocquelet)

By 2010, UNAMID included an engineering battalion from the 127th Light Mechanised Infantry Division of the People's Liberation Army of China. This brought to Darfur at least 12 WZ551/Type 92 wheeled armoured personnel carriers. Weighing up to 16 tons, these had a crew of three and could carry up to nine passengers. Their primary armament included a 12.7mm QJC-88/ZSL-92A machine gun. Additional WZ551s were supplied by Beijing to Zambian peacekeepers deployed with UNAMID, while four were procured by the Argentinean Army for service with the 12th Mechanised Infantry Regiment in Sudan. (Artwork by David Bocquelet)

Sudan acquired its first batch of Mil Mi-25D attack helicopters from Libya in 1989: throughout the following decade, these were reinforced through the acquisition of more than 20 Mi-24Ds, Mi-24Ps, and Mi-35Ps from Russia. Their deployment during the war in Darfur was very intensive and attrition heavy: the unit operating them – No. 3 Squadron, home-based at Jebel Aulia, south-east of Khartoum – never had more than about eight to 10 on operations at the same time. They were usually forward deployed at el-Geneina, el-Fasher, and Nyala in detachments of two or three, and frequently operated in combination with various marks of Mil Mi-8/17 assault helicopters. Principal armament was the twin-barrel 23mm autocannon installed low on the right side of the forward fuselage, and B-8 pods for 80mm unguided rockets. (Artwork by Tom Cooper)

Aiming to replace survivors of 24 Shenyang F-6 interceptors and two FT-6 conversion trainers acquired from the People's Republic of China between 1973 and 1983, in the summer of 2002 Khartoum acquired 12 Shenyang A-5C fighter-bombers from China (ASCC/NATO-reporting name 'Fantan'). Assigned to No. 24 Squadron, home-based at Wadi Sayyidna Air Base, north of Khartoum, they received serial numbers in the range 401 to 412. Only months later, the first few A-5Cs were observed forward deployed at el-Geneina, el-Fasher and Nyala airports, from where they operated not only against the insurgents, but flew attacks on numerous villages. Their primary armament consisted of the Chinese variant of the old Soviet-made ORO-57K pods for 57mm unguided rockets and 250kg free-fall bombs. (Artwork by Tom Cooper)

This is a reconstruction of one of about 20 Antonov An-26Bs acquired by the Sudanese air force since the early 2000s. They were regularly deployed to fly air strikes against insurgent-controlled villages in Darfur and earned themselves the notorious name of 'Antonov Bombers'. While usually assigned air force serials in the 7700 series, An-24s, An-26s, An-30s, and An-32s of the Sudanese air force often wore these in combination with civilian registrations: sometimes those of Sudan (prefixed 'ST-'), but at other times with fake markings identifying them as operated by foreign cargo companies. This example, active as around 2004–2010, was no exception: in addition to the air force serial 7705 on the fin, it also carried a fake registration on the rear fuselage. (Artwork by Tom Cooper)

The Janjaweed had their origins in the decades-long civil war gripping Chad and Sudan. In the 1980s, Libya began providing material support to the Arabic-speaking Abbala nomads of eastern Chad. The Sudanese government began enlisting them to counter Chadian incursions and then began deploying them to raid border villages in Darfur in the 1990s. By 2003, the Janjaweed functioned as a counterinsurgency force supplied with arms and communications equipment by the Sudanese military intelligence: they routed the SLA and launched a campaign of ethnic cleansing of the Fur, Masalit, and Zaghawa peoples, provoking an international outburst that led to the deployment of AMIS. Usually mounted on camels or horses, the Janjaweed in 2004–2006 typically wore BDU (battle dress uniform) fatigues in woodland pattern, while protecting their heads with typical white or dark green turbans (which were also often used to protect faces from the sun and sand). Many others wore the traditional *jalabiya*, a lose-fitting robe-like garment, often with a black baggy pocket or hood (called a *qob*) on the back. This raider is shown mounted on a Sudan Country-Bred horse, he has strapped a 7.62mm PKM machine gun on the right side of a light saddle positioned atop a thick woollen blanket. (Artwork by Renato Dalmaso)

Troops of the Rwandan contingent deployed with AMIS in Sudan generally wore the six-colour BDU desert camouflage uniform (often referred to as 'chocolate chip') drawn from US Army surplus. Made of a mix of polyester and cotton, this included a shirt with four front pockets and reinforced elbows, and pants with cargo pockets. This was usually completed by black leather combat boots – still something of status symbol within the Rwandan Defence Forces much of which was equipped only with rubber boots for all of the 1990s and early 2000s. The principal firearms were different versions of AK-47/AKM assault rifles. (Artwork by Renato Dalmaso)

Officers of the Hungarian Defence Forces assigned to AMIS wore their usual 1990M four-colour ('woodland') camouflage uniforms introduced in 1994. This included the M90 Army Shirt, black textile belt, summer field pants, and either M75 black leather boots or one of the more recent models. Standard headgear included a blue-coloured beret made of 100 percent wool, and having a black leather trim. (Artwork by Renato Dalmaso)

This lieutenant colonel of the Spanish Army (*Ejército de Tierra*) is shown wearing the six-colour BDU desert camouflage uniform that was standard in the US Army in the late 1980s and early 1990s. As usual for NATO armies, name tape and rank patches (usually in tactical brown, here in black) were worn above the left breast pocket, and the national flag on the left shoulder. (Artwork by Renato Dalmaso)

The Nigerian Army contingent of AMIS initially wore the Nigeria Army Camouflage Battle Dress in 'woodland' pattern, usually completed with a green beret and black leather boots. In 2005–2006, this was replaced by a new BDU uniform, predominantly in sand, with a camouflage pattern in olive green and dark brown. This were completed with ballistic helmets made of Kevlar, light blue vests with plate, and modern Gore-Tex boots in sand colour. (Artwork by Renato Dalmaso)

One of the best-equipped contingents to serve with UNAMID early on, was a company of 130 officers of the Indonesian Formed Police Unit (FPU). They arrived at Camp Garuda outside el-Fasher in December 2008, wearing Kevlar helmets in UN blue covers, fatigues in sand overall, plate carriers, cargo vests with ammunition pouches, knee pads, and armed with the then brand-new, indigenously developed PT Pindad SS2-V5 assault rifles, custom designed for short-range combat. (Artwork by Renato Dalmaso)

Map No. 4267 UNITED NATIONS
March 2006

Department of Peacekeeping Operations
Cartographic Section

A map of AMIS camps in Darfur, Sudan as of 2005–2006. (UN Geospatial Information Section)

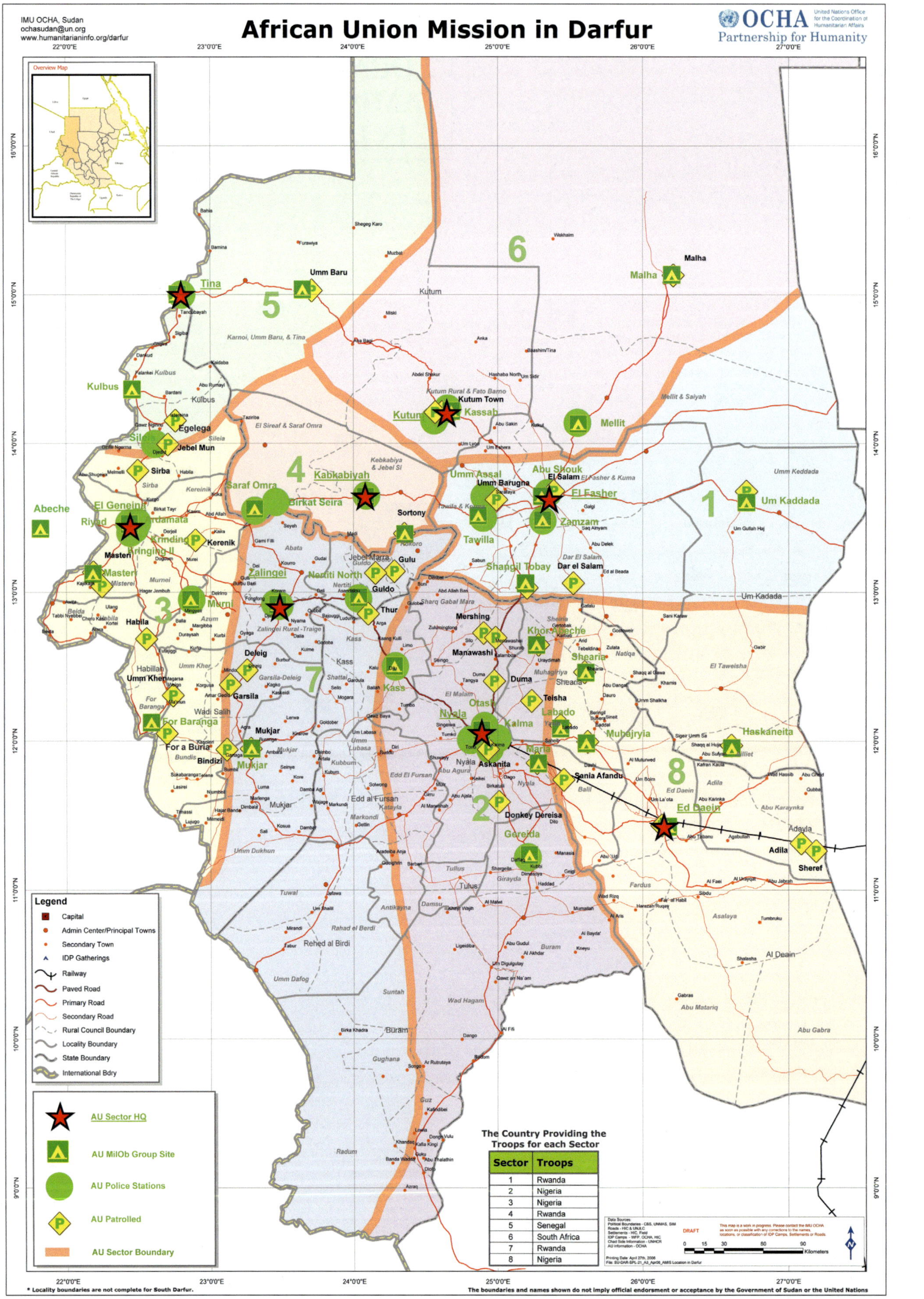

A map of major AMIS bases, patrol zones, and zones of responsibility for the different contingents as of 2005–2006. (IMU OCHA, Sudan)

Soldiers of the Nigerian Army contingent on a parade. (János Besenyő)

President of Sudan, Omar al-Bashir, during a visit to one of the AMIS camps in August 2004. (János Besenyő)

- 1 special (missionary) reserve company
- 3 special (sectors) reserve companies
- 1 company (headquarter-level)
- 2 logistic units
- 3 transportation companies
- 2 air-technical (helicopter) companies
- 1 military police company
- 1 ROLE II healthcare facility
- 120 military liaison experts
- 240 military advisers

The UN Department of Peace Operations wanted even more troops, and they expected the percentage of Africans in the mission to reach 50–70 percent. Even though the AU wanted to appear as the showrunners in the mission, in reality they were expecting the help of the UN for the mission to work better.[58] The date of the transfer of the mission to the UN was 1 January 2008, by which the organisation took over.

One of the Mil Mi-8 helicopters rented by the Canadian contingent from the private company SkyLink. (János Besenyő)

A pair of Mi-8s chartered from Russia, seen at Zalinge helipad in late 2005. (János Besenyő)

5
EUROPEAN UNION'S SUPPORT MISSION IN DARFUR

The EU was there at the beginning of the negotiations in the Darfur area, and it expressed its utmost commitment to the case and to persuade the Sudanese government. Besides that, they wanted to ensure closer cooperation between the world organisations and powers like the UN, AU, the Arab League, US and EU. Of course, their main goal was to help in solving the conflict between the Sudanese government forces and the rebels.[1] The organisation who wanted them to participate in the mission was the AU, and on 1 June 2004 they joined in. The EU helped with almost half of the mission costs which was approximately 12 million Euros.[2] Later, other types of assistance were requested from the EU too, because the AU was logistically not in control of the mission.[3] Th EU was thus willing to help in other ways too, and it sent the member states data about the mission:

- the EU would only assist, the leader was the AU
- the EU requests military experts, not simple soldiers
- the experts should remain for six months minimum
- some of the officers will receive leading positions
- the officers should be paid by the EU

With the main information shared, talks began with the EU member states. One observer became vice president for the Ceasefire Commission and 10 were sent to the AU mission in June 2004.[4] The states who sent military personnel to the site were Ireland, the Netherlands, Hungary, Sweden, Italy and Denmark,[5] and amounted to 10 persons.[6] The first problem was that neither the EU nor the AU had clear information about what was happening on the ground, thus they were not properly informed about the situation of the mission. In the beginning, this caused difficulties, until the vice president was appointed, and he started to manage these deficiencies. The EU soon realised that the AU was incapable of controlling the situation and the conflict as well, since 300 soldiers were not enough for a mission to be effective. Because the AU lacked the money it needed, the US requested that the EU help them in a letter addressing the following points:

- Was the EU willing to aid the operation?
- Advice for the EU to assess the areas in the mission that need support
- The US wanted the EU to head the AMIS so it could coordinate its logistical and financial tasks

To emphasise their commitment, the EU finally agreed upon extending their role in the operation. Talks were also held with the Sudanese government, and efforts made to undertake military tasks. After the arrangements, on 4–8 August 2004 the EU dispatched a delegation to examine the situation in Darfur. The proposed financial and military aid was handled carefully by the AU.[7] The EU Military Staff then issued a draft on 2 September 2004 that described in which matters the EU would assist AMIS.[8] After the AU's plan to enlarge the operation on 27 October the EU gave another 80 million Euros,[9] and further aid to the AU was planned.[10] Then the EU sent a list of advice to the AU organisation to help AMIS in December 2004.[11] On 12 January 2005 the AU and the EU started negotiations, and the EU members concluded the following issues:

- advisers dispatched to the conflict area
- useful data given to the AU
- forum arranged for further instructions
- EU liaison experts sent to the AU
- database of African soldiers trained in the EU
- expert group to be created to aid the AU
- the AU starts a training program for experts to be included in disarmament, demobilisation and reintegration issues

Altogether, the European Union was one of the biggest contributors of the AMIS mission. In 2004, the member states gave a contribution of 285.2 million Euros. Thus, the EU said that the problem was the deficit of proper equipment on the ground. By May 2005, the contribution to the AU missions reached 570 million Euros.[12] On other occasions, the EU negotiated with its counterparts – even Javier Solana – to give financial help to AMIS II. However, the AU was expecting more and more financial aid and the EU asked for patience, but the AU was adamant.[13] When money was lacking in 2007, the EU renewed its aid to AMIS with 100 million Euros, thus the EU was the saviour again.[14] By March 2006, the EU also gave an extra amount in the sum of 160 million Euros within the framework of the African Peace Facility. When the AU wanted to transfer the mission to the UN, they requested an additional 50 million Euros from the EU, which they got. The leadership of the EU called upon its member states to invest more in the AMIS peacekeeping operation.[15]

EU and NATO Air Proceedings

The problem here was the same as before: the AU lacked the proper supply of vehicles and machines to fulfil the mission's mandate. NATO, the US and EU financed solutions to these problems, but since NATO had the best logistic organisation it took responsibility for the largest part of the financing.[16] The air logistics of AMIS II were first discussed on 31 May 2005, in which the participants examined the details of the air system of the operation. Three issues

The wreckage of a utility car belonging to Save the Children, after it ran over a mine. (János Besenyő)

came up which could serve as a base for negotiations between the EU and AMIS. Firstly, a NATO executive offered a draft where the idea of a European Air Transport Command was raised. An additional organisation, the Combined Transport Centre (in Addis Ababa) was advised. The system would be directed by the EU, but the real transport would be a NATO task. Secondly, the system would be led by the EU command, and NATO would only have a marginal role. Thirdly, the leaders suggested a cooperative solution, where both the EU and NATO would have their organisational roles. At the end, the second draft was selected. Finally, a Joint EU/NATO Forward-Based Movement Cell was implemented in Addis Ababa and the EU took responsibility for its leadership, and cooperated with the AU force to secure the airlifts. The members of the EU created air groups, which worked together with the EU/NATO forces and thus handled the aerial issues. The country/organisation which financed the airlift had to handle the ground forces' organisation and the resource deployment as well.[17] The airlifts began between July and September 2005 with 5,857 persons dispatched by air to the conflict zone to extend the measures of AMIS II. Both EU and NATO planes carried African units, thus they helped AMIS in logistical issues. The due sums were financed by the biggest organisations and countries: NATO, UN, EU and the US. Since information flow was lacking in the mission,[18] the airlifts were not always without problems.

EU Logistical Experts

Because of a lack of experts in the mission, the AU president published a request on 31 December 2004 to its partners to ask for logistical help.[19] The AU wanted personnel for the following tasks:

- DITF: logistic expert, operations officer, etc.
- Mission Command: flight experts, financial experts, etc.
- Operation Command: communications officer, police officer, logistics officers, etc.

The AU wanted details about the job requirements and assurance of the qualifications of the officers.[20] Finally, the EU also wanted to send military observers, but it was not safe to do so.[21] The EU was hesitant to help the AU further because of previous differences and the mishandling of the money already sent. On 5 May, Germany and France published a proposal for the AU.[22] The EU knew that the AU needed more financial support, so they proposed a settlement plan:

- Dispatch of police advisers: the EU wanted to give military help to the AMIS police force, to Addis Ababa, Khartoum, el-Fasher, etc.
- Dispatch of military observers: the same as with police officers
- Airborne support for the AMIS mission: the transport of AMIS II units and soldiers was promised
- Logistic aid: equipment, vehicles and communication assessment
- Training and direction management: the capability enhancement of the African soldiers
- Aerial reconnaissance: aerial commodities offered by the EU to AMIS II. [23]

The AU was aggressively asking for more help and in May 2005 published a list containing the expected financial aid.[24] When the EU saw the list, they were surprised to see the amount of requested equipment and vehicles, but finally the EU leadership decided to let the individual states choose who would deliver what to AMIS, however, eventually the Military Staff decided. On 23 May 2005, the members negotiated and came to a conclusion that eight military experts should be dispatched to the operation,[25] and the equipment was also delivered. Due to the indifference of the AU military leadership, the head of the Military Staff, Major General Jean-Pierre Herrweghe wrote to the head of AMIS in which he advised him to decide if they need the equipment or not. Eventually AMIS decided to accept the items and the vehicles and arms were delivered.

On 6 June 2005, the EU Military Staff announced its reliance on the AMIS leadership and expressed the following:[26]

- the EU expressed its gratitude to AMIS and recognised that AMIS was difficult to maintain and offered its further help to assist the mission
- further aid to AMIS was required from the EU to enhance the mission
- logistical aid would be provided to AMIS in order to assist the mission's requirements
- EU experts were required to ensure useful cooperation between the EU and the AMIS operation
- a liaison unit should be created in Brussels to coordinate between the EU and AMIS organisations
- an airborne liaison unit of the EU/NATO was to be established in Addis Ababa to further coordinate transport between the EU and the AMIS operations
- the number of military experts in the AMIS mission was to be raised
- further development of the aerial reconnaissance in the conflict zone
- taking of responsibility for training African soldiers by the EU
- advice in order to develop the command forces of AMIS
- communication equipment needed to be given to the EU experts
- further financing of the AMIS mission
- information collection and utilisation for the EU Military Staff.

Overall, the EU knew that the AU and AMIS had either not enough resources or was not able to handle them well enough. Logistic aid was thus needed for the desired operation of the mission.[27] All of this resulted in the strengthening of the EU's standpoint that the AU and AMIS needed more experts and managers, but their transfer progressed slowly, thus the organisation reached the expected level only by September.[28] The next problem for the mission was the handling of the African experts and reaching the appropriate number of soldiers, which was completed by October–November. The ATHENA mechanism, in which EU member states – with the exception of Denmark – contributed funds to support the Common Security and Defence Policy, was used to finance the European advisers; however, the transport and other functions were carried out by member states.[29] Another issue was the leader of the organisation who had problems with the JLOC organisation, which he thought wanted to thwart his efforts. After the AU's mediation in the case, the issue was relaxed but the commander's feelings resulted in much confusion in the lives of the mission's experts, who tried to exclude the establishment from the leadership[30] and thwarted the creation of a Joint Operations Centre. Many divisive issues arose between JLOC and the AU, and there were many debates between the organisations. These were solved diplomatically, however, they remained present in the life of the mission. Since there were differences between the EU and AU officers, meetings were arranged to discuss the problems and the first was set up in May–June 2005.[31] The meetings were held regularly and the talks were quite fruitful by the end of the operation.

The EU Mission of Support in Darfur

The official start of the EU participation in the missions was on 23 June 2005 under the title 'European Union civilian-military supporting action to the African Union mission in the Darfur region of Sudan' and it aimed to help to coordinate the logistical realm of the AMIS mission. The ATHENA mechanism financed the mission.[32]

The next step of the EU was to delegate a special representative, Pekka Haavisto, who took care of the issues of the EU in the mission. He took part in the logistic organisation of the mission and also in the operational planning.[33] He also coordinated logistic talks with the Khartoum government and the AU-AMIS axis and took part in the Abuja Peace Conferences as well. The Addis Coordination Cell's duties were the following:

- coordination of the assistance of the EU member states
- coordination with Brussels
- coordination with the liaison officer in Addis Ababa and other military police officers
- coordination with AMIS donors (US, UN, NATO, etc.)

Since organisational matters were not in top form, to say the least, the EU sent a special military adviser, Colonel Philippe Mendez and a special police adviser, Superintendent Douglas Brand to the AU headquarters in Addis Ababa.[34] This way a special relationship was opened between the AU and the EU headquarters to receive information about the mission. The reporting system was functioning well by September 2005 and cooperation between the EU and the AU improved greatly. The European establishment thus created a new structure.

One of the major roles of the EU was to train the AMIS II officers. The lack of adequately trained policemen in Darfur was a serious problem for the refugees in the area who were practically in the hands of the peacekeepers. The police unit was not as trustworthy as expected, and thus the fate of the refugees was in danger. The police unit was aware of the following issues:

- distribution deficiencies
- lack of efficient policemen from African countries
- capability deficiencies
- police leadership was incomplete and inefficient
- lack of equipment and proper work circumstances[35]

A delegation sent to the conflict zone mentioned these problems and tried to enhance the training and increase the number of the police officers. On 26 May 2005, the EU therefore offered an additional aid package which was composed of the following, mostly police-supporting issues:

- improving the leadership of the police contingent
- supporting the training of the police personnel
- adding operational advice to help implement the ongoing plans

According to what had been arranged before, the AU was to assist logistically and otherwise for the unit of 49 EU personnel and three bureaucrats. Nevertheless, the EU still had to support its own officers.[36] Thus the EU had to provide the communications equipment since the AU was not prepared to fulfil its expected duties.[37] The problem for the EU was that the officers were hard to recruit and place, since the EU states were reluctant to dispatch more policemen familiar with the AU. Up to August 2005, just 22 persons were placed in the conflict zone. Thus Pedro Serrano, who was head of police matters, requested the member states to deliver more policemen.[38]

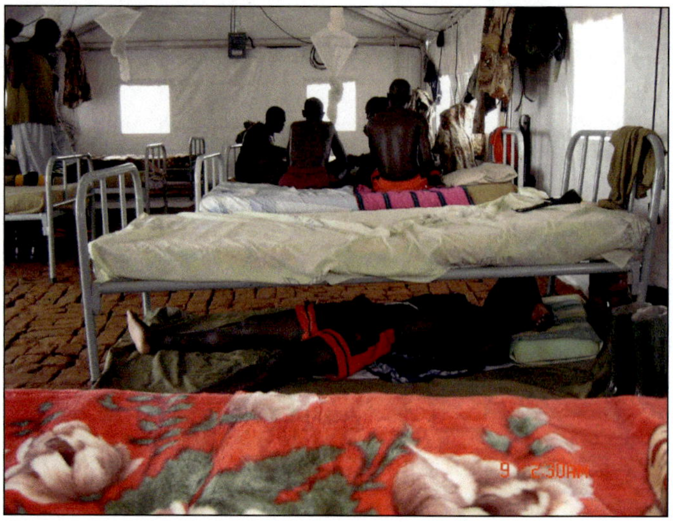

Soldiers resting inside one of their tents in the AMIS camp outside Mukjar. (János Besenyő)

According to Besenyő, there was a bigger problem: the arriving troops experienced bureaucratic problems, for the Khartoum government was not willing to allow the European police officers to participate in the mission until they received the proper Sudanese documents, despite the Addis Ababa Agreement of 28 May 2004 not mentioning such a prohibition against non-African units. Meanwhile, the situation on the ground deteriorated, and besides the Sudanese rebels' fighting against each other and the government, the Sudanese and AMIS leaders were reluctant to help the European troops and police, so the talks between the parties became more and more difficult to uphold. Even so, the Sudanese were continuing their murderous activities in the rebel areas.

The refugee situation became worse, the conflict remained and the circumstances had not changed very much, the European Union's Council dispatched a delegation on 16–22 September 2005 to examine AMIS II and its issues. Therefore, the committee assessed the situation and tried to convince the EU of further steps to enhance communications between AMIS and the EU.[39] The delegation negotiated with the AU, the EU advisers and the Sudanese government as well in each of the mission's centres, thus it became aware of the situation in the conflict zone. The African Union of course denied any accusation that the mission had deficiencies, and that it did not operate at full capacity. They stated that AMIS and the AU was fully capable of directing the organisation and they intended to continue to do so. Like before, they asked for more support from the EU states, and more military and police help. Their aim was to accentuate the African and AU leadership of the mission, try to minimise the European presence as much as they could and improve the financing of the mission.

The military leadership of the mission put great emphasis on the strengthening of the military contingent of the mission and highlighted the difficulties from which the operation and its logistics suffered. They wanted more troops on the ground to improve the effectiveness of the operation and they asked for financial help to make the mission more efficient. They also presented other problems: the logistic and organisational weakness of the AU leadership, which was – according to them – unable to hold together completely the mission and its forces.

The delegation missed the AU's acceptance of the advice of the advisers sent there in March 2005.[40] A lot of issues came up from the closing of the mission to the transfer of the operation to the UN. However, the main problem – according to them – was the financial deficit the mission was suffering, so they requested that the European states aid them with more support. The EU experts were critical of the mission; they emphasised the logistical, leadership-generated and operational deficiencies that practically devoured the mission. The leadership complained of lack of resources, for example in the food supply.

The PAE commander was very critical of the operation, and the lack of military and financial resources made the leadership wary of the mission's effectiveness. The European police officers also suffered from poor conditions. At the end, out of 1,560 policemen just 850 were dispatched to Darfur.[41] Notwithstanding the efforts of the policemen to improve their situation, the logistical and organisational problems were still present and because of that the operation was suffering from several issues.

There was then the issue of medical care. Colonel Michael Eger was one of the executive members who composed an assessment of the healthcare capabilities of the mission, and he was very disappointed in the results of his examination. The African medical unit was incapable of producing a normal healthcare aid for the peacekeeping officers who had to go to Chad, travelling 1,000–2,000km, for the nearest reliable hospital for treatment when they were ill. The training of the African peacekeepers and the medical equipment did not reach the appropriate level for the mission, so the soldiers had problems with the system. The problem increased when lower ranking officers were to be treated, since their healthcare was not handled appropriately by the leadership of the mission. The expert group assessed that because of these problems the EU wanted to renew its participation in three areas:

- political improvements to be achieved in coordination with the EU
- assistance with AU to be more successful
- assuring the quiet withdrawal of AMIS after a well-executed mission[42]

In 2006, the faltering AMIS mission required 100 million Euros from the EU, regardless of the expected transfer to the UN in 2006. In November 2005, another examination was carried out by the EU Military Staff about the conflict zone. They found logistical and organisational problems regarding the deployment of the peacekeepers. They criticised the communication with the Khartoum government, and they missed the honest relationship between the mission headquarters and the Sudanese leadership.

The Darfur contingent was also criticised: according to the report, the camps did not cooperate well with each other, the military observers were at odds with each other, and the command was not appropriate. The assessment also concluded that the expansion of AMIS was also not concluded, and the police officers sent from the EU were small in number, thus they advised the member states to provide more assistance to the organisation. Medical officers were especially needed. Of course, these problems were known by the EU countries, but because of bad experience they did not want to dispatch any more manpower or supplies.[43] Up to 2005, approximately 100 European peacekeepers had taken part in AMIS.[44]

To further the mission's goals, the EU Military Staff issued an enquiry on 24 November 2005 to its member states regarding the question of raising the number of participants in the mission. The countries were reluctant to help very much; Great Britain, Spain and Italy were not very keen to support the AMIS mission. Hungary even wanted to exit the mission's organisation, but the EU was insistent on increasing the numbers in the operation. To lift the spirits of the peacekeepers, the EU strived to develop conditions for the mission's participants.[45] Communication devices and housing were improved to make life better for the military observers.[46] There were also problems with pay for European officers, since while the AU officers got their money, the salary of the EU peacekeepers did not always arrive in time and thus created tension among the peacekeepers.[47]

There were other indications that the EU wanted to participate more in the AMIS mission, and they tried to enhance their role in the operation's activities but the number of military experts was not sufficient and more and more Europeans were leaving the mission. The spectacular exit of the European peacekeepers had an aversive effect: the EU decided to draft an extraction plan.[48]

The aforementioned events triggered the progress of the transfer of the AMIS mission to the UN, and the EU stood by the plan. Meanwhile, the Peace Treaty of Darfur was concluded, and thus the EU received a position in the Ceasefire Commission for the logistic-communication-financial organisation of the mission. This position became useful for the peacekeepers arriving with the AMIS mission later, who could turn for help to the officer in charge.

The AU also reorganised the mission's healthcare system by the time of the changes and gave responsibility for the healthcare of the officers to the arriving contingents. The centre of this medical system was el-Fasher, where the most important surgeries and other operations were executed.[49] The EU of course raised its concerns regarding the new AU system based on past experience. The lack of Nigerian healthcare personnel again pointed to the inability of the AU to organise the logistics of the AMIS mission.[50]

The initial reaction was to pull out the European personnel by 30 March 2006. The EU and the US then made a joint commitment that PAE would treat the 30 European experts.[51] The EU went further when they dispatched a medical team to Darfur in April 2006, who gave advice for the mission's healthcare.[52] The Europeans were so strict about health, that until the medical supplies were provided to the officers, they were not allowed to participate in the missions.[53] The EU was still not totally satisfied with these results, so in May 2006 a Swedish medical unit was dispatched to the conflict zone to improve the capabilities of the African personnel, thus the Europeans were safer as well.[54]

There were still other problems, as some of the African officers were showing hostility to the European advisors and military observers, and in Addis Ababa the situation deteriorated.[55] The AU however was quite content with these results and thus eventually a Forward Joint Mission Headquarters was set up. The contingent was also fully staffed with police and civilians.[56] At first, the EU wanted to order home its peacekeepers, but later they changed their minds and an extra 32 experts arrived.[57] On 18–20 June 2006, a conference was organised in Brussels to exchange past mission experience between members, and everybody who had been a member of the Darfur contingent could participate.[58] The conference was very useful, since the experts who took part were able to give advice from which the members learned a lot about the ongoing conflict and the mission.[59] The EU was helpful in other ways too, because it also provided logistic, financial and legal experts to help the AMIS mission.[60]

Troops of the Nigerian Army in their field kitchen. (János Besenyő)

Nigerian soldiers washing their clothes. (János Besenyő)

A high-ranking military expert from the EU, Colonel Francois Amelineau, reported that the EU still maintained its support to the AMIS mission at the beginning of 2007, nevertheless there were some deficiencies in the mission since their advice was not always taken seriously. According to Besenyő, their logic was based on the 'African way' of thought and was why AMIS and the Africans were so reluctant and sometimes hindered the European efforts. Soon the UN had to start to intervene to improve the situation, and in February 2007 they dispatched 47 military officers and 30 police experts to strengthen the AMIS mission. However, the logistics were problematic, and the main issue was poorly organised catering: AMIS wanted to distribute food rations and they expected financing from the Europeans, and finally France was good hearted enough to help.[61] The new special representative of the European supporting mission, Torben Brylle, wanted to withdraw the European experts of the AMIS mission after the UN took responsibility for the operation.[62]

The head of the EU Military Staff, Lieutenant Colonel Ronald Dorenbos went to the conflict zone in Darfur between 18–20 June 2007 to examine the situation on the ground, and he was surprised to find the European experts in harsh conditions. However, the soldiers were in good spirits and they were happy considering their living standards. Dorenbos observed that the African leadership of AMIS did not fully cooperate with the EU staff since they tried to exclude the Europeans from some of the positions. They were excluded from parts of the mission's program, but they were at the same time expected to work well.[63] In el-Fasher, the situation resembled the previously mentioned problems. The African mission commander wanted the Europeans to cooperate and do their jobs well, but he and his advisers did not let them participate in the mission's main talks. He said he needed only the Africans to complete the duty at hand.[64]

Nevertheless, the Europeans tried to live up to the expectations of their supervisors in the mission and do a good job notwithstanding the hinderance of the Africans. While the military contingent struggled with problems regarding integration, the police officers had no such problems with their African counterparts and they fitted into the mission very well. There was a sad event when an Egyptian man killed somebody in the neighbourhood of the Europeans in Khartoum, but the Sudanese reacted, so the Europeans could move back to their houses after the incident. The lieutenant colonel however reported that even though the EU was giving a lot of aid to AMIS, it had become ineffective by that time and it was the UN's turn to supervise the operation.[65]

6 HUNGARIAN PARTICIPATION

In the first years of the AMIS mission, in 2004 the AU requested from other international organisations help for their mission, and among others, Hungarians took part in the logistic and financial part of the operation. First, one officer was dispatched from the country.[1] Hungary was always ready to help AMIS, and since its initiation the country's troops were ready to move in if needed. Its political leader understood well that the Darfur conflict was an important affair and the press was very interested in it.[2] Instead of the first thought, that Hungary should give more financial aid, the country sent one military observer, Major Ferenc Kajári, who arrived in Darfur on 29 July 2004. Nevertheless, financial contributions were also on the list, thus the following was given to AMIS:

- Ministry of Foreign Affairs: 40,145 Euros
- Ministry of Defence: 5,842 Euros
- UNICEF Hungarian National Committee: 40,145 Euros
- Hungarian Ecumenical Charity: 8,029 Euros
- Total: 94,161 Euros

Furthermore, the Hungarians were generous to give more aid to the crisis area including Innomed Medical Ltd endowing medical equipment to the AMREF charity organisation participating in AMIS missions.[3] The coordination of the mission's activities went to Colonel Tibor Kovács on 22 October 2004 via the Ministry of Defence.[4]

Nevertheless, the EU observers were officially not part of the AMIS mission, but the EU considered it necessary to deploy them, and since they were regarded as unofficial from time to time, their positions, ranks and tasks were sometimes unclear. They were thus maltreated or not positioned according to their official rank or occupation, and there was every now and then a little confusion regarding their role in the AMIS organisation. At first – since the EU dispatched mainly retired, high ranking officers – they could not find a proper job, and they were weary of 12–14-hour patrols in the desert. The AU contributed greatly to this by disregarding the European officers because of the aforementioned matters. This was not the case with Major Ferenc Kajári, who – because of his high skills – was sent to Kabkabiya camp to serve as a reconnaissance expert. He sometimes did voluntary work by writing reports and organising issues by himself, which was much appreciated. It is worth mentioning that the Africans acknowledged European observers only from Hungary and Italy.[5]

There were other problems that made the situation more difficult in the AMIS operation, since the AU expected the EU officers to be fully trained and the EU vice versa, but neither of the two organisations' officers was fully trained for such a mission and this presented difficulties. Fortunately for the Hungarians, Major Ferenc Kajári was aware of the logistical issues in the mission so he came prepared. The worst problem was the lack of logistic supply and thus the officers could not start their work in time. Major Kajári went in July 2004 to the fourth sector and they were without supply until October. The equipment and the logistics were in bad condition, and the mechanisms that should have operated the camp were insufficient. Nevertheless, by the end of October, the camp's basic institutions were functioning. It was created for 70 persons but by May 2005 approximately 300 persons were accommodated in the camp. In spite of the harsh circumstances, it was also planned that the civilian police contingent would be deployed by that time, however, there were insufficient supplies in the sector.[6]

Other problems also thwarted Major Kajári's service, as the well in his camp dried out, thus the logistical circumstances of the mission became harder. Since the mission was led by the AU, the UN – to which Major Kajári belonged – did not count as much as the African organisations. The situation was due to the lack of organisation by the Africans in the mission area. For the officers, language knowledge was a must. English was widespread, but the problem was that the Africans knew French.

Nevertheless, the Kabkabiya camp was in the area of the fighting that happened in Darfur between the sedentary rebels and the Janjaweed, and so it was not a very safe place for peacekeepers. On 7 March 2005, an attack occurred in the vicinity of Sharif Umra village when assailants shot at the AMIS personnel. Tents were hit but the officers survived the incident.[7] In conclusion, it can be said that the report of Major Ferenc Kajári proved that the situation on the ground had not improved, and the insecurity could be felt around the camps of the Darfur area. He witnessed the Sudanese government's forces cooperating with AU personnel against the rebels. Noting the lack of signatures from rebels and militia leaders on the ceasefire agreement, AU military experts were not immune to the rebel forces and at times they attacked them. Thus, AMIS had to dispatch a security company to protect its soldiers from militia and rebel attacks.

Major Kajári also reported the improper communication equipment and the lack of useful information for the peacekeepers. He also pointed to the poor level of language knowledge of some of the officers in the mission. Because of these circumstances, the idea of withdrawing the Hungarian major was raised but the expectation of better organisational and logistic support was more promising, so the mission continued with the Hungarian officer in place. Eventually, the Hungarian presence was prolonged and the replacement for Major Kajári – although it was not an actual issue – was a possibility.[8]

Coauthor Besenyő preparing for a patrol with troops of the Rwandan Defence Force contingent and one of their RG-31 Nyala MRAPs. (János Besenyő)

Although the beginning was difficult for Major Kajári, by the end of his time serving at the camp it was functional and more organised. The communication system was improved thanks to the Hungarian government, but the laptops provided often malfunctioned because of the great heat, so Major Kajári did not store his data on the computer. The major finally advised the Hungarian military leadership to provide better equipment in the future.[9] One of Major Kajári's biggest contributions to the international mission and the Hungarian Defence Forces was that he wrote a resume about the mission's details which was very useful.[10] His writings inspired one of the authors of this book, János Besenyő, who later served as a logistics expert in the mission. Major Kajári was nevertheless so acknowledged among the peacekeepers, that he was invited to hold a course for the AU peacekeepers.

When Major Kajári finished his duties on 26 July 2005, the EU wanted to send an observer and a logistics expert as well. The latter was a must, since the AMIS mission was not operating well logistically, thus the supporting organisations (EU, NATO, UN, etc.) wanted to ensure the proper functioning of the logistical side of the operation.[11] The logistic experts were then decided upon, and the member states sent officers to establish an appropriate logistics system in the camps and to assist in the organisation of AMIS III as

Participants of the NATO-organised course in el-Fasher, in September 2005. (János Besenyő)

well. As usual, the AU wanted to remain in control, and wanted to send one officer to the side of the European officer to tell him what to do.

Hungary was reluctant to dispatch more officers but had no choice, because the EU wanted more. At the end, the logistics position was in question,[12] and finally a Hungarian logistics expert was advised to be sent. It was not easy to find a suitable logistics expert because the old, experienced officers did not want to participate, so the Hungarian Defence Forces finally chose János Besenyő, one of the authors of this book, to be their logistics expert in Darfur. His abilities were perfect for the job, as he served in Western Sahara as catering chief and deputy chief of the logistic system, thus he was accepted.[13] When the training for the mission was over, Besenyő arrived at Addis Ababa on 29 June 2005, and without further orientation, the work started at once. The mission documents were a priority and the experiences of previous officers were then studied. In Addis Ababa, they served under Ambassador Ki Dougaye, and the Ethiopian Mesfin Binega. Besenyő – as previously mentioned – recorded the events in his diary (7 July 2005):

> For the time being we are in the headquarters of AU in Addis, where we get new tasks from day to day. They are rather kind of "fire-fighter" tasks, and projects which should have been done long ago. Several signs show that here the NATO, EU and AU representatives are not fully synchronised; each of them says something different related to us. Compared to the original plans, we are already late; we are supposed to be at the operational field by this time, not at the headquarters. According to the Africans, European advisers are not really needed and it is enough if we are here for only three months. By contrast, the EU's local representative, a German Colonel Reinhard Linz plans up to six months. The European colleagues are very helpful. I think there will be no problem with each other. As the representatives of the United Nations in Ghana, Major General Henry Anidoho was informed that I am a food supply officer; he called me into his office. He would like me to help solve the problems of camp hygiene and nutrition, of course, besides my original job as deputy head of the Field Support Service. Almost immediately he called the mission commander, a Nigerian major general to take care of me. Well, I do not know how well you are taken care of... especially when the majority of Africans are already suspicious of us, whites. According to Major General Anidoho, who started as a simple soldier, even Africans claimed that the quality of food is very low and in many camps overcrowding and lack of hygiene regulations could trigger epidemics. The major general has a very strong opinion on almost everything. He said that he is one of Kofi Annan's friends and that he was the deputy commander of the peace operation in Rwanda – on which events he also wrote a book.[14] The general's attention can be good and bad, too. For now, I follow the advice of the French colonel Jean-Luc Charrie, I carry out all the work I am given and I am as flexible as possible. Now the AU began a new battalion's deployment, in which we also must take the lion's share because the MOVCOM personnel are not sufficient for the task, so we will probably need to work in Nyala, as the Nigerian battalion is deployed. Apparently, it won't be an easy game, because the camp can only accommodate 300 people, but now 485 Nigerian soldiers arrive, plus all the equipment and ammunition for one year.[15] The same is true for the other camps, as the Africans definitely want to show success in their first independent military mission. The African officers are still nowhere (as far as we know they are not even nominated!), so only we work now and everything we need to create, we create it from scratch. Almost every day we get to bed around midnight,

The AMIS camp outside el-Fasher during the rainy season. (János Besenyő)

Besenyő stands next to a patrol car in the flooded AMIS camp outside el-Fasher. (János Besenyő)

Flooded JLOC office in the AMIS camp outside el-Fasher. (János Besenyő)

> but the next morning we get up at six o'clock already. But I do not complain, because it is a newly created organisation.
>
> The operational field is relatively calm, but the Sudanese army detained one of our patrols in free movement, so they returned to the camp. Because of the decision of the Sudanese authorities, Nyala airport cannot be used for delivering Nigerians as part of the airlift, so they are sent to el-Fasher, then to Nyala by car. Although we tried to look for other solutions, it is almost one hundred percent sure that only the car should reach the Nigerians' second sector. In addition, during the rainy season the roads are impassable! In sector one, tribal clashes took place between Zaghawa and Masalit tribes, but the good news is that 153 civilians returned to the villages, which have lived in refugee camps. Almost every day I read the mission reports (those, which I can receive because of the lack of functioning communication), and almost all I can read is a set of problems... It seems we're going to work properly for our salary. Last night we tried to get to Khartoum, but the Ethiopian Airline sold more tickets than the actual number of seats, so there was no room on the plane. Tonight we will try again. If we fail, maybe we can travel on Monday. NATO officers assured me that this is normal here.[16]

Besenyő and the other officers were eager to go to the mission area, but first they had to get training in Khartoum, to be prepared for the operation's tasks. In the end, the leader of the Addis Liaison Office, Dr. Wilfried Asombang welcomed him into the mission, but informed him that he was a guest and since there were many colonial sins, he should repent his sins, and he was made aware, that this is Africa, where the Europeans are not the leaders, and he should keep these thoughts to himself. Besenyő reacted by saying that Hungary was never a colonising country, thus we had only peaceful intentions. The African officer said he would keep that in mind but let him be suspicious for the time.[17] Nevertheless, the following day Besenyő arrived at Operation Headquarters in el-Fasher.

The awaiting conditions were depressing, since there was only temporary accommodation, and there was no time to accommodate the mission's needs. The logistic section of the operation was deficient; there were not enough officers and those there were had who had poor training.

Besenyő had to begin immediately in the 'Sleeping Bag' operation. The name of the mission was ironic, because it referred to the poor conditions the 5,000 peacekeepers would face when they arrived at the camps. Since the operation was the AU's first really independent mission, it had to function perfectly, to show that the AU was capable of such operations and to prevent the UN from taking over.[18] The logistic deficiencies of the mission and the lack of capability of the AU enabled them to call for more troops and logistics experts and since without the international organisations they could not function, they required their help in that.

One of the problems was that the actual commander of the mission was never present, so the logistical leader had to take responsibility for the issues at hand until Besenyő and the logistical experts arrived at the scene. When the Hungarian and other officers arrived, they had to work immediately; there was no room for acclimatisation. Besenyő and his colleagues started the work at once and set up a thorough logistical draft for the mission camps which were delivered to them. At this point, the logistics experts faced the difficulties of the mission: there was no common mechanism for the planning and the joint work stuttered. Also, there was the problem of the African experts' behaviour towards work and Europeans, which made things not so easy for Besenyő and his fellows. Their thinking was somewhat strange, because they listened to what the Europeans had to say, they listened to their advice, but then they did not usually carry out the expected tasks, and waited for their European counterparts to do the hard work, and they thought that it was their job to finish the issues at hand. There was a lot of confusion: first, the Africans told Besenyő and his colleagues that the mission commander at the scene arranged everything, then the commander came and told them that he did not do the required work, since he was the leader. Besenyő decided that it was better to take matters in their own hands.

One patrol started with a mistake, since none of the drivers and participants were present at the discussion in the morning, so the visit had to be postponed to the next day. Thanks to heavy rainfall, the desert had become difficult to cross. After a difficult trip, Besenyő arrived in Tawila camp. The intention was to house 209 Rwandan peacekeepers, but one can imagine the circumstances: there were no kitchens, beds or mattresses, etc. There were problems with the other camps next to the present one, so it was difficult to accommodate everybody's needs in the conflict zone. Besenyő and his compatriots could not move, because the air transport was impossible due to lack of fuel and the roads had not dried up yet, so they had to wait. Despite the weather and other logistical problems, after the drying up of the desert they could move out and complete their mission, and to Besenyő's satisfaction they were able to house the Rwandan soldiers at the end.[19] Air transport was difficult due to the aforementioned conditions and the distrust of the Africans towards the Europeans.

An entry from Besenyő's diary on 21 August 2005:

> I describe the current situation only briefly; it would be enough of a word. Sometimes I feel we can't sink any lower than this. If the AU and the leadership of the mission will not pull itself together, not only won't they increase the number of personnel by 12,000, but bankruptcy proceedings shall end the entire AMIS career. This week, the local provider ceased operation of telephone and fax lines due to unpaid bills. In the camps there is not enough food, clean, safe drinking water, malaria and acute diarrhoea are almost daily problems. It had been five days that the camp has not received food because of the lack of fuel. Helicopters are unable to fly and the roads are impassable in the rainy periods. The JLOC excluded itself, they made us do everything and everyone blamed us for everything. In addition, there is this NATO-UN MAPEX exercise, in which we participate. The camp was flooded again by the rainwater and the wastewater from the city. Dead animals are lying in several places of the camp. Neither I nor my British colleagues could sleep because our bed was flooded. We asked for shelter from the Swedish communications officer, who lives in one of the highest parts of the camp. He reaches only knee-deep in the water... There is no internet; my cell phone from home was not working, because there is no roaming agreement between Hungary and Sudan. The only good point of the day was that I made onion cream soup and pizza for us in the kitchen. Thus, for the first time in weeks I am pretty happy with the food.[20]

Besenyő continued in his diary as follows on 28 August 2005:

> In the recent period we continued the deployment of African battalions through the NATO air-bridge and participated in the MAPEX exercise organised by the UN, NATO and the USA. The exercise finished today. During the week, in the second sector (Nyala), one of our patrols was attacked. One Nigerian soldier got shot in the leg. After the late MEDEVAC (there is not enough fuel for the helicopters to operate), the soldier was immediately operated on and now he is in stable condition. Overall, the activities of the armed rebel groups seem to intensify, while government forces only protect the most important settlements. Moreover, the Janjaweed groups and sometimes also the government's military and police departments carry out attacks against the residents of the refugee camps, raping girls and women who are heading to get water or collect firewood became "common practice".
>
> Delivery of the Canadian APC vehicles will begin in mid-September, the operating units (10 Canadian officers, non-commissioned officers) will arrive on 10th September in el-Fasher.
>
> We constantly have problems in almost all areas, there is not enough equipment, vehicle, tent, and what is most important, very few well-trained, competent African logistics specialists. Therefore, we "the whites" are literally overworked. Our African partners have still not arrived, works of different components are uncoordinated and there is no unified logistics management. I'm sleep-deprived, tired, upset that we need to discuss everything with Africans, who are suspicious towards us and do not believe that our work is beneficial. Sometimes I feel almost like „Kőműves Kelemen"[21]... Who do I have to build in to move on?[22]

Besenyő and his crew carried on organising the logistics of the camps, and they were able to dispatch 5,323 military officers, 534 policemen and they supplied equipment and ammunition and set up 57 convoys.[23] Despite that the main organising belonged to the JLOC of European and African officers, the EU/NATO air corridor troops also helped in executing the aforementioned plans.

Nevertheless, Besenyő was the Field Support Service deputy commander whose duty was to handle the logistic duties and the camp resources, besides writing reports to his supervisors in the mission about his work. In the following part we assess his personal experiences in these fields.

An Ilyushin Il-76TD transport chartered from the United Arab Emirates' company Experts Cargo to support the AMIS contingent in Sudan. (János Besenyő)

An Antonov An-28 light transport, chartered to support AMIS operations. (János Besenyő)

Field Support Service[24]

Besenyő regarded the food supply as his main task, and he took part in its organisation with real enthusiasm. The system was twofold, because on the one hand the US company PAE got the servicing job, but on the other hand, a Sudanese company, AMZAR became responsible for the feeding of the soldiers. The AU organised things in its own way again, as the subcontractors wanted from African countries did not have qualified experts, thus those filling the ranks of the logistics were mostly untrained. Nevertheless, after a while they adapted to the circumstances of the organisation of the supply. However, the main supply was carried out by the new logistics centre, who informed civil companies about their duties. The food supply or catering was a major problem, since almost all of the mission commanders lived outside the camps, and they neglected this area of supply.

There was a lot of organisational confusion, for example, the menu was not up to date, there was no checking on the food supply, and some of the chefs were unqualified. Thus, Besenyő started to organise the catering. The first thing he did was to issue a questionnaire about the food: the results were mixed, the officers mostly complained about the monotony of the food, only rice, beans, etc. The portions were not very satisfying either. The organisation of the canteen was not so good, as there were endless lines, a lot of waiting and the food was not very diversified.

So Besenyő took matters in his hands and wrote a resume to the Head of Mission General, after which negotiations took place between the sides, and long talks were held about the issues at hand and the catering. Finally, his modifications were mostly accepted. Besenyő had compiled a recipe book on his Western Saharan mission in which there were approximately 300 recipes, which was taken in by the AU and accepted as the official guide for the mission and was sent to the 32 camps. The next step was the creation of a menu with a US marine 'Uncle Denis', thus the catering started to look better and better.

There were, however, other duties that Besenyő performed during his time serving in Darfur: he had the opportunity to meet with members of the Khartoum government and the UN Mission in South Sudan. There was an interesting negotiation that took place on the occasion of the death of Sudanese Vice President Mebior Garang, which caused several incidents. Besenyő recorded them in his diary once again, as follows:

> This morning in Khartoum street fighting broke out between supporters of Garang and the police. The AMIS headquarters was surrounded, sparse shooting could be heard. No getting in or out of the headquarters was possible. Flights between el-Fasher and the capital were cancelled. The local Sudanese liaisons are not willing to give info. According to the SLA representative, anything could happen. Soon we got to know that John Garang, Sudan's vice president, former opposition SPLA [Sudanese People's Liberation Army] leader died in a plane crash while travelling home from a meeting in Uganda. Since there is no authentic person who could follow the successor, the peace process is at risk, and internal party struggles are expected. This may include revived fights in the south. According to the locals (JEM, SLA and even, according to some local interpreters!) it is likely that President Bashir ordered Garang's plane to be blown up. Of course, no evidence proves this, but this can base some opposition media or organisations that so far have refused to sign an agreement with the government and only suspended fighting because of the fear from SPLA. Garang's deputy is a Jikany Nuer, Riak Machar, who is supported by the Nuer tribe, but the Dinkas oppose him. Garang's deputy from the Dinka tribe did not acquire the support of the Shilluk and Nuer tribes. Hopefully, the four Hungarian peacekeepers, which have been offered to South Sudan UN operations, will stay home for a while... Seemingly for this afternoon the situation returned to normal in Khartoum, though we can see smoke at several places at the outer districts and gunfire is still heard. The AMIS headquarters did not suffer any offensive, but the police clashed with a group of demonstrators nearby. The AMIS leadership was on alert but warned the rest of the observers and civilian employees to calm down. The Sudanese "military observers" are still not in the headquarters and the SLA "observers" also left the headquarters.
>
> At the HQ's restaurant, we watched the Al Jazirah channel with Cypriot and Spanish colleagues, Major Panayiostis Aresti and Lieutenant Colonel Jose Sanz Alvarez. As they speak Arabic, we can't understand anything, even though the images can tell it all. Later, I saw that a dead body was taken from the street. The channel broadcasted this several times and, in the background, a large column of smoke could be seen. Mission leaders do not have real info, so a number of [versions of the] news spread in the headquarters.[25]

After the normalisation of the situation, Besenyő went back to el-Fasher. Because some of the officers wanted their own national food, the logistical crew created a separate kitchen where they could cook for themselves.

Another issue came up, since the hygiene of the kitchen was poor, and it needed reformation. Besenyő lived up to the task, however, his regulations were not kept in order after he was absent from the scene. There were stories about the Hungarian giant (Besenyő is tall) who collected food in jars: they did not get the point that Besenyő was checking the quality of the supplies. Eventually, even the persistent logistics officer had to accept that this was not Europe and he could not create hygienic conditions as they are there.

He also struggled with the logistic organisation of food supplies. Food did not arrive at the camps since there was a lack of fuel in the mission,[26] and the leaders of the operation did not care very much about the catering logistics of AMIS, which made it very difficult for Besenyő and his crew to organise the proper food supply.

According to Besenyő, of the required 120 tons of food he was happy if he received half of that quantity. He also recorded his thoughts on the theme in his diary on 28 October 2005:

> The quality of food is slowly improving and we get more and more ingredients, but it is still hardly enough. This week we received "only" 88 tons out of the needed 120 tons, but in the past four months, it was still the best week. There were weeks when we got 35.5 tons instead of the required 120 tons. The mission leaders were pointing at the PAE, their leaders at the AU. It is almost impossible to solve why we can't receive the ordered amount of food in the camps. Tomorrow Colonel Matz [has] scheduled a meeting where EU advisers, AU's logistics and PAE representatives will also be present. I hope it will make sense. Meanwhile, the new teams keep coming. More than 7,000 troops are here now. It seems that South Africa will not send [a] battalion because it is not able to provide sufficient trained people (three companies and medical division in Burundi, two companies in Ivory Coast, two companies and medical division in Liberia, two companies in Darfur, including a technical and a demining unit) and they are fed up with the fact that they are the greatest – almost the only – contributors of the AU. Whatever happens, it is sure, the only hard-hitting unit was sent by South Africa, which would also be able to operate either independently. Unfortunately, we can't tell the same about the other nations' soldiers.[27]

Besenyő noted that – as the diary entry shows – it was difficult to handle catering. The situation went on until the UN joined the mission. Since there was a lack of refrigeration capability, Besenyő thought it would be wise to put together at least 50,000 food packs. At a JLOC negotiation, his advice was respected. Consequently – and to Besenyő's surprise – the AU asked for 207,508 food packs to be sent by the EU, and this was because the commander thought the Europeans were rich anyway… It seemed that Besenyő's request was taken too seriously… Nevertheless, this caused difficulties for the food logistics.[28] The events were recorded by the logistics officer as follows:

> The AU has officially asked the partners, including the EU countries, to provide the mission a total of 208,000 combat ration (MRE) packages. According to my calculations, up to 50,000 kits are required. In my opinion, the AU wants a kind of security reserve, as they aren't able to deliver enough fresh food to the camps. Based on preliminary discussions, the British, the French and the Americans are ready to offer these packages to the AMIS. I asked the ones at home, but somehow we are not interested in this topic. Finally, issued by the Slovenian army, 1998 ready meal kits arrived, the French also sent 18,000 sets and the Americans offered 300,000 sets. Unfortunately, the proper storage for the time being has not been solved, but we are working on a solution.

It will require a significant amount of money (constructing a safe, constant temperature warehouse).[29]

Eventually, the volumes requested by the AU were given by the British, French, the US, South Africa, Danish and Slovenians. The Slovenes however gave pork meat, which was not halal… Nevertheless, the Muslims also got their portions as time passed by. Because the logistic planning was not well executed by the mission leaders, in June 2006, the food resourcing was a misery again, which resulted in the appeal of the commanders for 17,640 meals, which should have been delivered by France.[30]

Eventually, Besenyő's service was a success, as the food supply organisation improved a lot during his stay in the mission. The commanders wanted to prolong his stay in the operation, but the Hungarian leadership called him back from Darfur due to their lack of faith in the operation's future, thus Besenyő stayed until December 2005.

Lieutenant Colonel Jose Sanz Alvarez, logistical adviser at the AMIS command in Khartoum. (János Besenyő)

Water Resources[31]

Water was also very important for the mission, and PAE was at the head of its distribution. There was an expert, who examined the quality of the water supply, but serious testing was done only in matters of urgency. Nevertheless, the situation concerning the wells was poor, since they were almost all contaminated by waste material, or they were too salty to drink from. Because the correct Reverse Osmosis machinery could not be bought for the camps to purify the water 40–50 percent of personnel frequently had diarrhoea. Besenyő tried to acquire bottled water but he was unsuccessful, and the water available for cleaning and other personal use was not suitable to drink since it was contaminated. They tried boiling water for drinking it but that was also not completely useful. Diarrhoea was a constant phenomenon, and people became sick and/or were sent to hospital. Besenyő himself experienced a 40°C fever and diarrhoea in a difficult situation where no drinkable water was available. These incidents were reduced by far when the UN took over the mission.

Besenyő's experiences were difficult, since only 19 out of 32 camps even had a well supply, drilled by PAE and supervised by AMIS. The other camps had to maintain contracts with civilians living nearby and because of droughts, wells dried out and sometimes this caused problems between the officers and the civilians. Despite the successful negotiations between the parties, the peacekeepers and the SLA and others fought again for water.[32]

The drought was solved with help from the villages all around. Only a reduction in the number of the officers took place.

Officer's mess in the AMIS camp outside Nyala, in November 2005. (János Besenyő)

Organisational Build-up of Camps[33]

Besenyő thought of this area of the mission as the hardest problem to solve, but since the logistics officer's job consisted of organising, he was able to get around the problem. At the beginning, 24 camps were set up in the whole mission area, which was the same size as France, but when Besenyő was called back, 33 camps were functioning, albeit overcrowded. The main work was done by PAE, who organised basically every aspect of the camps' everyday life. It should be mentioned that the AU contribution to camp management was poor, and by itself it could not maintain the functioning of the sites.

Besenyő was in charge of a 57-person logistic unit in each camp, the Combat Support Unit, but the Africans deployed in the units lacked logistic expertise and their language skills were poor. Although Besenyő was in charge of the operations, in reality, PAE helped him greatly with the organisational efforts. There were problems with the placement of camps, as they were sometimes built in high-risk areas. For example, el-Fasher in the rainy season was under 50–60cm of water. Besenyő recorded these events in his diary on 15 August 2005:

> I had never seen such a huge storm and a rain shower that reached us on 12th, August. At three o'clock AM the walls of the tent were fully wet so we pulled the beds to the middle of the room, hoping that at least the rain wouldn't reach our back. We tried to sleep but could not, because we heard more and more shouting. So I thought I'll look what happened. However, when I left the bed, very sobering experience hit me, as shin-length water covered the floor. I woke up in a moment ... When I stepped out the door, I saw a few South African soldiers right away who tried to dig a channel between some tents with shovels [and] axes. Two tents further,

A truck with local PAE workers. (János Besenyő)

African policewomen tried to carry out the water from their tent in smaller and larger vessels, but at least three times more flowed back immediately. The water carried trash and all kinds of military equipment between the tents. One of the policewomen tried to collect her clothes from the torn drying-line, but the clothes were scattered all over. I managed to save one of the clothes out of the muddy, dirty water, and then tried to hand over more elegantly. The policewoman looked at me somewhat amazed. I noted that I am fully covered with mud. In comparison to me, even a wet sparrow looks more like a gentleman... I laughed, and then everyone went on their separate ways. After that, we dug channel all night long to drain water. British Major Adrian Garside and I joined the South Africans, but the majority in our tent was just looking at our torture. They wouldn't ever leave their bed... In the morning we only had ankle-depth water left, so before I went to have breakfast, I tried to secure my equipment as far as it was possible. However, most of my clothes soaked up the dirty water and smelled like a sinkhole ... I put everything on top of my bed, and then went to have a breakfast, hoping to get a hot tea after the night. Towards the dining room, a devastating view greeted us everywhere. Almost knee-height water remained in the canal, which washed the waste water out, and we saw several dead animals in it. Some tents collapsed and soldiers tried to gather their things from the ruins. Then we arrived at the canteen, which was also under water. They told us that they can't give tea, and not much else because the kitchen is flooded, so they gave us combat rations. From there we grudgingly went to our office in a container, which was also under water. Some counsellors were standing there already, wondering how to get into the office, when Colonel Quba arrived, who said that we should not work until the water lessened. I asked him how I can send the food to the camps now. He replied that even the airport is under water and none of the planes will take off. After that, we went back to the tents, twisted our clothes and hung them to dry. We could not wash because the laundry was flooded and all the washing machines were destroyed. Although we did not get more rain, it took three days for the water to dwindle, and for us to be able to do anything in our camp. In the offices, all computers, phones, furniture were ruined... Until now, no deliveries could happen, as dirt roads are impassable, and only now could the airport start operation again, because due to the high water, Matthew Petroleum Tankers could not get into the airport with the fuel supply. Fortunately, I have no time to complain, because so much work was torn on us that at night we just fell in our bed and slept...[34]

The camps were organised poorly, and new housing was almost impossible to fit in alongside the other tents. The story was not a pretty one, for negotiations took place between the sides, since the Sudanese government thwarted the expansion of the camps and there were land disputes between the peacekeepers and the locals, which resulted in hostilities. The result was that the peacekeepers had to proceed cautiously with the enlargement of the sites. Along with the African soldiers' unrealistic wage expectations, the AU raised the number of soldiers by 5,000, and the reader can imagine what kind of hygienic, housing, catering problems this caused in the camps. For example, el-Fasher was created to accommodate 250 people, but in September 2005, Besenyő needed to provide housing for 700. With the camp enlargements, life got better by far in the camps. However, by December 2005 the goal was to build new camps besides the existing 33, which was impossible to execute financially.[35]

The operational method was the following: every camp had a PAE leader, who organised things. If there was a problem, he reported to the mission headquarters. Here the head of Field Support Service checked the problems, and the logistics expert implemented a solution, which was then checked by Besenyő by visiting the sites.

The 'Red Sea' facility for water purification. (János Besenyő)

Nyala airport in autumn 2005. Note the four Mil Mi-8 helicopters of the UN contingent, several light liaison aircraft and a civilian Boeing 707 airliner (background right). (János Besenyő)

Fire Service Organisation[36]

The number of fires was due mostly to cooking by the Africans in their tents. The officers were not so reliable in this line of work, so PAE and AMZAR had to do the bulk of the work. Thus, Besenyő and his crew organised a fire security protocol to reduce such cases. According to the plan, every camp got a fire marshal who was responsible for these matters. The fire equipment was continuously checked on.

Hygiene Coordination[37]

This was the responsibility of a South African group, Medical Support Solutions, but they did only medical tasks. The real job was to be carried out by the Force Medical Officer. The role was divided: Besenyő concentrated on the kitchen, while the overall hygiene circumstances of the camp fell under PAE jurisdiction. Besides the Sudanese garbage cleaners, a camp health officer was in charge of the sanitation at a site. They and the PAE experts examined the water purity as well.

The End of the Hungarian Participation in the AMIS Mission

Despite the satisfaction of both the AU and the EU with Major Kajári's and Besenyő's work, in October 2005 news spread that the Hungarian participation might be closed down. Notwithstanding, Besenyő's liaison officer requested him for a six-month prolongation, to which he agreed. However, Besenyő's duty eventually expired on 27 December 2005, and the Hungarian leadership did not plan on prolonging the mission time. Lieutenant General László Braun reported to Major General István Talla (Hungarian Military Representative to NATO headquarters in Brussels):

Major Adrien Garside, of the British Army, serving as a JLOC member in el-Fasher. (János Besenyő)

> I inform you that regarding our further participation in AMIS II operation – after consultation with the Ministry of Foreign Affairs and the Ministry of Defence Department for Defence Policy – the following decision was made. Hungary does not intend to maintain the participation in its current form in the African Union Mission in Sudan, so after the expiry date, 25th December, we do not extend the currently deployed officer's mandate. However, in the future – if the opportunity arises – we do not exclude ourselves from the different forms of participation in the AMIS operation.[38]

Despite this, the Hungarian participation was not completely forgotten,[39] but the Congolese involvement was more important to the Hungarian leadership at the time. Thus, the Hungarian mission came to an end. Eventually Besenyő received an honour for the operation at a consultation on 19–20 June 2006 from the EU Military Staff.

7 CONCLUSION

The book's aim has been to describe the situation in Darfur and to give an insight to the AMIS mission and the Hungarian experience related to it. We hope the book was able to provide additional information thanks to the personal mission experience of coauthor Besenyő. This conclusion will be about assessing the book and its consequences.

Firstly, the conflict in Darfur formed step by step, and the violence that had many roots, including ethnic, religious, and colonialism, became more intense due to the actions of the Sudanese government and al-Bashir from 1989, who disregarded the rights of the Darfurian sedentary farmers.[1] Because of its 'non-intervention' policy, the African Union did not want to intervene, but since there was strong pressure from other organisations, it took up a mediatory role, then slowly engaged in peacekeeping activities.[2] The largest problem was the lack of ability of the AU to finance its own operation, thus the UN and other organisations had to step in. It was only as a result of a US oil embargo that the Khartoum government sat down at the negotiating table and reached an unstable agreement with the Darfurians. The other issue was that the AU continuously wanted to secure its leading position in the mission, but it had to rely instead on the help of the UN, US and EU. It wanted a mission without the help of Europeans, but it needed their financial contribution.[3] Thus the AU was very sensitive about the mission since it was a demonstration of its capabilities, thus it thwarted international interference.[4] From the beginning, AMIS was a deficient mission, because it lacked the proper equipment, resources and training to create a functioning operation. The AU needed aid from the EU member states and the UN, but it often disregarded their requests. They also changed the implementation of Rwandan and Nigerian troops which caused confusion in the logistics of the mission. The AU required the assistance of its counterparts for the implementation of the handling of one million displaced persons. AMIS relied on international aid until the end of its operation.

The Khartoum regime however thwarted the mission's success in many ways, hindering issuance of visas and thwarting the actions of the peacekeepers. The dispatched Sudanese experts obstructed the prosecution of the Janjaweed which caused several problems. With this, the Sudanese lost a lot of respect in the eyes of the rebels, thus they turned away from the help of the observers.[5]

The mission was not very effective, due to logistical problems, and problems with the number of peacekeepers. The change of the mission structure in October 2004 did not have a lot of effect. In fact, the conflict became more intense and the idea of pulling AMIS out was raised, however, this was not realised due to political and diplomatic reasons. Nevertheless, because of the small numbers and ineffectiveness of the AU mission it resorted to increasing the number of its troops up to 3,320 persons.[6] However, the expansion of AMIS was not very successful, due to logistic problems and that manpower was still insufficient.[7] The AU therefore made an effort to increase the number of soldiers, but they lacked the required linguistic skills. The problem was that for the AU this was a matter of African pride, thus they did not want to expel the unqualified officers, and that caused logistic and other kinds of difficulties in the mission.

The extended operation, AMIS II, thus failed to live up to expectations because of the aforementioned issues. There were also problems with intelligence, communication and other areas.[8] The rebels sometimes also attacked the peacekeepers, and the devolving security environment caused distrust among civilians towards the mission.

AMIS II was for these reasons an incomplete mission by 2005, and it still struggled with the same problems AMIS I had, like logistics deficiencies and the need for more resources. It was thus not surprising that the wider world wanted a UN takeover, but the AU rejected the idea, and the extension of AMIS II into AMIS III was decided by raised manpower. The issue was the strengthening

Rwandan and Nigerian soldiers dancing during a break. (János Besenyő)

Troops helping move a patrol car out of the mud. (János Besenyő)

Refugees in the camp outside al-Sharif. (János Besenyő)

of capability of the operation, and to continue to observe and handle the security issues more delicately.[9]

Nevertheless, the same issues reappeared, as the military component was too small, the logistics were not well organised, and the worsening situation in Darfur was making the resolution of the conflict difficult for AMIS III personnel. The increase in the number of personnel and the lack of proper logistic organisation always came up and thwarted the proper execution of the goals of the mission.[10] Notwithstanding that the AU saw the problems, it still wanted to be self-reliant. Thus, at the end of 2005, they made efforts to prolong the operation. The AU planned to raise the number of soldiers by 4,000, so the mission's capabilities would amount to 12,300 persons, however it lacked realisation. Nevertheless, because of the logistic and financial deficiencies, and the sometimes-late payments, AMIS III still struggled with problems.[11]

The issues were still evident by 2006, and it could be seen that the operation suffered from several difficulties, which were not remedied by the extension of the military capabilities. The situation on the ground in Darfur was still dire, and the peacekeepers were still unable to solve the issues at hand. The AU had the same problems, and – as Besenyő thinks – the three years of efforts to achieve the missions' goals seemed to be ineffective. A UN takeover was again raised, and the Africans started to realise that maybe it was an option to be considered.[12] Nevertheless, since the AU was not willing to enhance its mission but wanted rather to rely on foreign aid, the transition to the UN was postponed by two years.

The transfer was completed finally by UNSC Resolution S/2007/468, and the legal basis of the creation of a hybrid force of AMIS and the UN was given, thus UNAMID was authorised.[13] The plans made clear that the act would be concluded on 31 December 2007, and the number of participants would reach 19,555 persons. After that, AMIS became passive, and only waited for aid and the takeover. The importance for the AU was that the mission would stay 'African', and European peacekeepers were not advised to participate in the new operation. The final year of AMIS was also dysfunctional, due to logistics and the aforementioned reasons; meanwhile, negotiations were neglected between the sides which made it difficult for the situation to improve. Even the mission's leaders knew that they depended on foreign aid and without the help of the international financial budget, their efforts would have been in vain. So they wanted to rely on the EU and its partners to help them with the implementation of the mission. The operation's success was thus not assured very well.[14]

It was clearer and clearer that the optimism of the AMIS and AU efforts was not well-grounded, and the lack of equipment, weak training and the confused command issues were going to lead to the operation's breakdown. There were hostilities between the government, the rebels and the peacekeepers, who were not let into certain areas of the conflict zone, thus they rather just waited and did not do anything, and so the mission stalled. In fact, there were projections that even the future AU-UN hybrid mission would not have a very bright future. However, in the end, the UNAMID hybrid operation was created on 1 January 2008.[15]

Although the AU wanted to show the world it was capable of such an operation, it was clear that its efforts were unsuccessful, and this was due to the reluctance of the AU to accept help from other organisations such as the UN to lend their experience to make their mission more effective. Had the AU cooperated with the UN sooner, they would have been rather more successful than the way it turned out when they tried to do everything by themselves.[16]

The EU was also negatively affecting the mission's outcome. Their fault was that despite knowing that the mission was dependent on them and was not very successful, they still poured money into it without critically thinking through the situation. The organisation started its assistance after the N'Djamena accords. They tried to act as mediators between the Sudanese forces and the rebels. Besides supporting the African way of thinking, they inspired the other major international organisations to aid the mission the way they were able to.[17] Nevertheless, the EU wanted to give payment in packages rather than in small amounts. In 2004, the AU asked for the aid of the EU, which it gave to them that year to the amount of 12 million Euros.[18] Although the EU also wanted to send experts alongside the financial aid, this was not realised due to the reluctance of its members.

Refugees in the camp outside Abu Shok. (János Besenyő)

Another scene from the refugee camp outside Abu Shok. (János Besenyő)

Troops of the Rwandan Defence Force contingent leaving Sudan in same fashion in which they arrived: on board a C-130 Hercules transport aircraft of the US Air Force. (János Besenyő)

The EU was keen to delegate officers and experts to the mission: in June 2004, the EU sent an officer to the AU Ceasefire Commission with the rank of Deputy Chief of Staff, and not so much later 10 military officers were dispatched to Darfur. The EU also handled a liaison officer in Addis Ababa. However, there was a feeling of mistrust from the Africans, and the EU experts did not get the daily reports or information about the mission.[19]

From July 2004, the European Union yearned to carve a bigger piece out of the pie but its members hindered the efforts, as they concluded bilateral agreements with the Africans rather than acting unanimously. This was also a negative issue for the mission in Congo (Artemis) where the member states contracted their own deals.

After that, in October 2004 the AU thought of expanding the mission, which was helped by 80 million Euros from the EU.[20] In December they even collected data for the AU so that they could use the documents for further improvement.[21] The EU was so generous with the AMIS mission that it supported a total sum of 285.2 million Euros of regional financial aid. Despite the funds being improperly used many times, the EU continued to finance the mission, and by May 2005, 570 million Euros were given to the conflict zone for further support.[22] As late as 2007, the EU gave 100 million Euros for maintaining the operation's existence.[23] The EU was even more generous as it also distributed money for the AU via the African Peace Facility, and when the takeover of the UN was agreed on, they helped the transition of the program.[24] Nevertheless, NATO was asked to conduct the airlift option since the EU had no such military capabilities. However, the cooperation between the EU and NATO was not always smooth because of several smaller problems which were prevalent through the operation.[25] The EU sent a lot of financial aid for logistic equipment too, but since the Africans lacked knowledge regarding this support, the EU wanted to dispatch consultants too. There were two problems: the member states were not eager to deploy the experts because of previous bad experiences, and the AU received them with suspicion, so the equipment was not used properly and the number of officers was usually not enough.[26] The EU therefore created an operation to support AMIS on 23 June 2005: this was the European Union's civilian-military supporting action to the African Union Mission in Darfur region of Sudan. By September 2005, the new mission became intertwined with the AMIS operation, and the EU also supported AMIS with police forces to complete its staff.[27]

Unfortunately, the AU did not take into consideration the advice of the European experts and the funds given to the organisation were further not used for appropriate reasons. For several reasons some of the leaders of the EU wanted to withdraw from the operation, but others thought that without the EU the mission would break down. That is why they stayed until UNAMID was deployed.[28]

Hungary took part in the operation from the beginning, because it correctly thought that the mission had huge international support and thus the country could have gained much from joining the operation. Finally, Hungary sent one military observer for a year from 2004 to 2005 to the Darfur mission.[29] The preparations were not perfect though, because the Hungarian officer did not receive previous instructions and at the mission area the European officers were not always treated according to their rank. Both the EU and the AU waited for the other to prepare the officers for the operation.[30]

The logistics system was also deficient, so Besenyő was dispatched as a logistic expert after the first officer had the same difficulties. After witnessing the logistical catastrophe in the area, Hungary wanted to pull out, but the EU made them stay because they thought Besenyő could make a difference if he concentrated on the task. After these negotiations, Besenyő was dispatched to the Darfur zone as a logistics consultant. Besenyő made every effort he could, and at the end, the mission's logistic system became well organised. The AU and the EU were so satisfied that they wanted him to stay a half year more, but the Hungarian government pulled him out and ended their presence in Darfur. Unfortunately, the Hungarian experiences were not regarded as important at that time by the leadership, and even though the Hungarian policy changed towards Africa and it became interested in the continent, the Hungarian Defence Forces have not developed an understandable Africa draft. According to Besenyő, because of several reasons, including political, economic and military, Hungary's presence in the zone is necessary, so revising the experience collected by the peacekeepers would not only help the military, but also the politicians and higher-level bureaucrats. Besenyő's opinion is therefore that the information gathered about the missions in Africa should be systemised more thoroughly, and the authors hope this view has been presented in this book as well. However, further research is advised on the theme.

BIBLIOGRAPHY

Archival Sources:

3000/COMJCL/023/07 - HM-HIM HL MH Separated Assortments, 80/AMIS – Sudanese mission

74-4/ 157 /2005/EU - HM-HIM HL MH Separated Assortments, 79/AMIS – Sudanese mission

African Union Darfur Integrated Task Force, Weekly Report No. 16., 16. August to 12 September 2005, 6-7. - HM-HIM HL MH Separated Assortments, 77/AMIS – Sudanese mission

African Union Darfur Integrated Task Force, Weekly Report No. 16., 16. August to 12 September 2005, 9. - HM-HIM HL MH Separated Assortments, 77/AMIS – Sudanese mission

African Union, *Agreement with the Sudanese Parties on the Modalities for the Establishment of the Ceasefire Commission and the Deployment of Observers in the Darfur,* Addis Ababa, 2004, https://peacemaker.un.org/sudan-darfur-ceasefire-commission2004, accessed 04 February 2023.

African Union, *Briefing Note on the renewal of the mandate of the AU Mission in the Sudan (AMIS) - PSC/PR/2 (XLII),* Addis Ababa, 2005, http://www.peaceau.org/uploads/reportmandateeng.pdf, accessed 13 February 2023.

African Union, *Communique of the 46th. meeting of the Peace and Security Council - PSC/PR/Comm. (XLV),* Addis Ababa, Ethiopia, 2006, https://reliefweb.int/report/sudan/sudan-peace-and-security-council-46th-meeting-communique, accessed 27 February 2023.

African Union Report *of the chairperson of the commission on the status of the implementation of the Peace and Security Council decision of 10 March 2006 on the situation in Darfur and the conclusion of the Abuja Peace Talks. PSC/MIN/2 (LI),* Addis Ababa, 2006, https://reliefweb.int/sites/reliefweb.int/files/resources/26CC3D0F09E665B085257171007003F2-au-sdn-15may.pdf, accessed 06 March 2023.

African Union, *The African Union and the conflict in the Darfur region of the Sudan. Meeting the challenges of peace, security and stability, CONF/PLG/3(I),* Addis Ababa, 2005, https://reliefweb.int/sites/reliefweb.int/files/resources/A0AD919C2B396D0FC125700D004A49AC-au-afr-26may.pdf, accessed 04 February 2023.

AMIS II mission, 3/353/2005 HM-HVKFH, 25. November 2005. - HM-HIM HL MH Separated Assortments, 78-I/AMIS – Sudanese mission

AMIS II Movement Update - 24 August 2005 - HM-HIM HL MH Separated Assortments, 77/AMIS – Sudanese mission

AMIS III. background, organisation - HM-HIM HL MH Separated Assortments, 80/AMIS – Sudanese mission

AU Led Joint Assessment Report, 20 December 2005. - HM-HIM HL MH Separated Assortments, 78-I/AMIS – Sudanese mission

AU request for advisor's PSD/DITF/NV/1869 - HM – HIM HL-MH Separated Assortments 75/AMIS – Sudanese mission

Briefing by Dr. Salim Ahmed Salim, AU Special Envoy and Chief Mediator for the Darfur Conflict, to the U.N. Security Council on 13 January 2006. Speech presented at the UN Security Council. - HM-HIM HL MH Separated Assortments, 78-II/AMIS – Sudanese mission

Broad options for NATO support to the UN mission in Darfur - HM-HIM HL MH Separated Assortments, 78-I/AMIS – Sudanese mission

CCD 07-00/03 OPS 195/04 HM-HIM HL MH Separated Assortments, 78-I/AMIS – Sudanese mission

Colonel János Besenyő's unpublished diary of Darfur. (Darfur: 2005).

Committee on Foreign Relations United States Senate, *Darfur revisited: the international response: hearing before the Committee on Foreign Relations United States Senate. September 28, 2005.* U.S. Government Printing Office, 2007, https://www.foreign.senate.gov/imo/media/doc/092805_Transcript_Darfur%20Revisited.pdf, accessed 04 February 2023

Council Joint Action appointing a Special Representative of the European Union for Sudan, Brussels, 13 July 2005 - HM-HIM HL MH Separated Assortments, 78-II/AMIS – Sudanese mission

Council Joint Action on the European Union civilian-military supporting action to the African Union mission. In the Darfur Region of Sudan - HM-HIM HLMH Separated Assortments, 77/AMIS-Sudanese mission

Council of the European Union. 2004. Action Plan for ESDP support to Peace and Security in Africa 10538/4/04. REV. 4. Brussels, 16. November 2004, https://data.consilium.europa.eu/

doc/document/ST%2010538%202004%20REV%204/EN/pdf, accessed 13 March 2023.
Darfur – EU Support to AMIS, DG 205/05 - HM-HIM HL MH Separated Assortments, 80/AMIS – Sudanese mission
Designation of Hungarian Point of Contact, 207/PSC/Fax/2004. - HM-HIM HL MH Separated Assortments, 79/AMIS – Sudanese mission
Details on the delegation and the submitted opinion: UN Security Council, *Report of the Security Council mission to the Sudan and Chad. S/2006/433,* 2006, https://reliefweb.int/report/chad/report-security-council-mission-sudan-and-chad-4-10-jun-2006-s2006433, accessed 06 March 2023.
DGEUMS visit to Sudan/Darfur 18-20 June 2007 - HM – HIM HL MH Separated Assortments, 78-I/AMIS – Sudanese mission
Draft Concept for EU Civilian/Military Supporting Action to AMIS II - HM-HIM HL MH Separated Assortments, 78-I/AMIS – Sudanese mission
Draft Council Conclusions – Sudan/Darfur, Brussels, 27 October 2004 - HM-HIM HL MH Separated Assortments, 78-II/AMIS – Sudanese mission
EU meeting of AMIS deployed EU MILOBs and technical planning experts, IM 07-07/03 DG 188/05 - HM-HIM HL MH Separated Assortments, 80/AMIS – Sudanese mission
EU MSR weekly report – Week 04/2007 - HM – HIM HL MH Separated Assortments, 78-II/AMIS – Sudanese mission
EU MSR weekly report – Week 21/2007 - HM – HIM HL MH Separated Assortments, 78-II/AMIS – Sudanese mission
EU MSR weekly report – Week 23/2007 - HM – HIM HL MH Separated Assortments, 78-II/AMIS – Sudanese mission
EU MSR weekly report – Week 26/2007 - HM – HIM HL MH Separated Assortments, 78-II/AMIS – Sudanese mission
EU Observer for the Ceasefire Commission in Sudan/Darfur – IM 07-07/03 DG 396/06 - HM-HIM HL MH Separated Assortments, 79/AMIS – Sudanese mission
EU Organisation Arrangements to Manage the Consolidated Package of Support to AMIS II - HM-HIM HL MH Separated Assortments, 78-I/AMIS – Sudanese mission
EU Organisation Arrangements to Manage the Consolidated Package of Support to AMIS II - HM-HIM HL MH Separated Assortments, 78-II/AMIS – Sudanese mission
EU Organization Arrangements to Manage the Consolidated Package of Support to AMIS II - HM-HIM HL MH Special Collection Documents, 80/AMIS – Sudanese mission
EU weekly report, Monday 28-May-07 until Sunday 03- Jun-07 - HM-HIM HL MH Separated Assortments, 78-II/AMIS – Sudanese mission
EUSR MA weekly report – Week 04/2007 - HM-HIM HL MH Separated Assortments, 78-II/AMIS – Sudanese mission
EUSR MA weekly report – Week 05/2007 - HM-HIM HL MH Separated Assortments, 78-II/AMIS – Sudanese mission
EUSR MA weekly report – Week 06/2007 - HM – HIM HL MH Separated Assortments, 78-II/AMIS – Sudanese mission
EUSR MA weekly report – Week 10/2007 - HM-HIM HL MH Separated Assortments, 78-II/AMIS – Sudanese mission
EUSR MA weekly report – Week 14/2007 - HM-HIM HL MH Separated Assortments, 78-II/AMIS – Sudanese mission
EUSR MA weekly report – Week 15/2007 - HM-HIM HL MH Separated Assortments, 78-II/AMIS – Sudanese mission
EUSR MA weekly report – Week 16/2007 - HM-HIM HL MH Separated Assortments, 78-II/AMIS – Sudanese mission
EUSR MA weekly report – Week 17/2007 - HM-HIM HL MH Separated Assortments, 78-II/AMIS – Sudanese mission
EUSR MA weekly report – Week 19/2007 - HM-HIM HL MH Separated Assortments, 78-II/AMIS – Sudanese mission
EUSR MA weekly report – Week 20/2007 - HM-HIM HL MH Separated Assortments, 78-II/AMIS – Sudanese mission
EUSR MA weekly report – Week 21/2007 - HM-HIM HL MH Separated Assortments, 78-II/AMIS – Sudanese mission
EUSR MA weekly report – Week 23/2007 - HM-HIM HL MH Separated Assortments, 78-II/AMIS – Sudanese mission
EUSR MA weekly report – Week 25/2007 - HM-HIM HL MH Separated Assortments, 78-II/AMIS – Sudanese mission
EUSR MA weekly report – Week 26/2007 - HM-HIM HL MH Separated Assortments, 78-II/AMIS – Sudanese mission
EUSR MA weekly report – Week 27/2007 - HM-HIM HL MH Separated Assortments, 78-II/AMIS – Sudanese mission
EUSR MA weekly report – Week 29/2007 - HM-HIM HL MH Separated Assortments, 78-II/AMIS – Sudanese mission
EU weekly report, Monday 26-Feb-07 until Sunday 04-Mar-07 - HM-HIM HL MH Separated Assortments, 77/AMIS – Sudanese mission
Extension of our Hungarian military observer presence in Sudan, 230/PSC/EM/05, 27. April 2005. - HM-HIM HL MH Separated Assortments, 79/AMIS – Sudanese mission
Fact Sheet: EU Response to the crisis in Darfur, Brussels, 10th June 2004 - HM-HIM HL MH Separated Assortments, 78-II/AMIS – Sudanese mission
FJMHQ AMIS – IM 07-07/03 DG 347/06 - HM-HIM HL MH Separated Assortments, 79/AMIS – Sudanese mission
German/French non-paper, Sudan/Darfur: Proposals for an enhanced role of the European Union - HM-HIM HL MH Separated Assortments, 78-II/AMIS – Sudanese mission
Great Britain: Parliament: House of Commons, International Development Committee, *Darfur: The Killing Continues; Second Report of Session 2005-06; Report, Together with Formal Minutes, Oral and Written Evidence,* The Stationery Office, 2006.
HIM HL MH Separated Assortments, 76/AMIS – Sudanese mission
HM-HIM HL MH Separated Assortments, 75/AMIS – Sudanese mission
HM-HIM HL MH Separated Assortments, 77/AMIS – Sudanese mission
HM-HIM HL MH Separated Assortments, 78-II/AMIS - Sudanese mission
HSP Joint Military Strategic Concept and HSP Police CONOPS.
IM 07 – 07/03 DG 082/06 - HM – HIM HL MH Separated Assortments 78-II/AMIS – Sudanese mission
IM 07 – 07/03 DG 101/06 - HM – HIM HL MH Separated Assortments 80/AMIS – Sudanese mission
IM 07 – 07/03 DG 208/06 - HM – HIM HL MH Separated Assortments 80/AMIS – Sudanese mission
IM 07 – 07/03 DG 253/06 - HM – HIM HL MH Separated Assortments 78-II/AMIS – Sudanese mission
IM 07 – 07/03 DG 261/06 - HM – HIM HL MH Separated Assortments 78-II/AMIS – Sudanese mission
IM 07 – 07/03 DG 271/06 - HM – HIM HL MH Separated Assortments 80/AMIS – Sudanese mission
IM 07 – 07/03 DG 304/06 - HM – HIM HL MH Separated Assortments 80/AMIS – Sudanese mission
IM 07 – 07/03 DG 315/06 - HM – HIM HL MH Separated Assortments 78-II/AMIS – Sudanese mission

IM 07 – 07/03 DG 365/06 - HM – HIM HL MH Separated Assortments 78-II/AMIS – Sudanese mission

IM 07 – 07/03 DG 383/06 - HM – HIM HL MH Separated Assortments 78-II/AMIS – Sudanese mission

IM 07 – 07/03 DG 496/05 - HM – HIM HL MH Separated Assortments 78-II/AMIS – Sudanese mission

IM 07 – 07/03 DG 498/05 - HM – HIM HL MH Separated Assortments 78-II/AMIS – Sudanese mission

IM 07 – 07/03 DG 510/05 - HM – HIM HL MH Separated Assortments 78-II/AMIS – Sudanese mission

IM 07 – 07/07 CCM 024/06 - HM – HIM HL MH Separated Assortments 78-II/AMIS – Sudanese mission

IM 07-07/03 CCM 012/06 - HM-HIM HL MH Separated Assortments, 80/AMIS – Sudanese mission

IM 07-07/03 CCM 027/06 - HM-HIM HL MH Separated Assortments, 78-II/AMIS – Sudanese mission

IM 07-07/03 CCM 046/06 - HM – HIM HL MH Separated Assortments, 78 – II/AMIS- Sudanese mission

IM 07-07/03 CCM 077/06 - HM-HIM HL MH Separated Assortments, 78-II/AMIS – Sudanese mission

IM 07-07/03 DG 022/06 - HM-HIM HL MH Separated Assortments, 80/AMIS – Sudanese mission

IM 07-07/03 DG 193/06 - HM-HIM HL MH Separated Assortments, 78-II/AMIS – Sudanese mission

IM 07-07/03 DG 272/06 - HM-HIM HL MH Separated Assortments, 78-II/AMIS – Sudanese mission

IM 07-07/03 DG 296/06 - HM-HIM HL MH Separated Assortments, 80/AMIS – Sudanese mission

IM 07-07/03 DG 314/06 - HM-HIM HL MH Separated Assortments, 80/AMIS – Sudanese mission

IM 07-07/03 DG 348/06 - HM-HIM HL MH Separated Assortments, 80/AMIS – Sudanese mission

IM 07-07/03 DG 362/06 - HM-HIM HL MH Separated Assortments, 80/AMIS – Sudanese mission

IM 07-07/03 DG 368/06 - HM-HIM HL MH Separated Assortments, 78-II/AMIS – Sudanese mission

IM 07-07/03 DG 397/06 - HM-HIM HL MH Separated Assortments, 78-I/AMIS – Sudanese mission

IM 07-07/04 DG 317/05, Brussels, 22 July 2005 - HM-HIM HL MH Separated Assortments, 78-II/AMIS – Sudanese mission

IM 07-07/07 CCM 079/06 - HM-HIM HL MH Separated Assortments, 78-II/AMIS – Sudanese mission

IM 07-07/07 CCM 083/06 - HM-HIM HL MH Separated Assortments, 78-II/AMIS – Sudanese mission

IM 07-07/07 OPS 112/05 - HM-HIM HL MH Separated Assortments, 78-I/AMIS – Sudanese mission

IM 07-07/08 OPS 098/05- HM-HIM HL MH Separated Assortments, 78-I/AMIS – Sudanese mission

Information Note to the Political and Security Committee (PSC) on the Requirement to Amend the 3rd Contribution Agreement with the African Union (AU) on the Financing of the AMIS Operation in Darfur from the African Peace Facility (APF)

Information Paper on possible EU military implications in the light of the Action Plan for ESDP support to Peace and Security in Africa, IM 01-16/20-07 OPS 212/04 - HM-HIM HL MH Separated Assortments, 78-II/AMIS – Sudanese mission

Information Paper on Sudan/Darfur and AMIS EUMC 2 February 2005 - HM-HIM HL MH Separated Assortments, 78-I/AMIS – Sudanese mission

Interview with a member of Darfur Integrated Task Force, who insisted on his anonymity

Interview with an EU adviser, who served at Darfur in this time and who insisted on his anonymity

Interview with members of AMIS II mission, who insisted on their anonymity

Interview with some EU advisers and military observers, who insist on their anonymity

Javier Solana welcomes today's appointment of Pekka Haavisto as EU Special Representative for Sudan, Brussels, 18 July 2005 - HM-HIM HL MH Separated Assortments, 78-II/AMIS – Sudanese mission

Manning of the FJMHQ – IM 07-07/03 DG 348/06 - HM-HIM HL MH Separated Assortments, 79/AMIS – Sudanese mission

Meeting Note Sudan/Darfur, 2004. June 28, 1. - HM-HIM HL MH Separated Assortments, 77/AMIS – Sudanese mission

Meeting Note Sudan/Darfur, 28 June 2004, 1. - HM-HIM HL MH Separated Assortments, 82/AMIS – Sudanese mission

Military Advice on the draft Action Plan for ESDP support to Peace and Security in Africa, Brussels, 2 September 2004 - HM-HIM HL MH Separated Assortments, 78-II/AMIS – Sudanese mission

Monthly Report EUSR Sudan – April 2006 - HM-HIM HL MH Separated Assortments, 78 – II/AMIS - Sudanese mission

Monthly Report EUSR Sudan – May 2006 - HM-HIM HL MH Separated Assortments, 78-II/AMIS – Sudanese mission

NATO Military Liaison Team in Addis Ababa – Weekly Sitrep 16/07, covering period 12 - 20 April 2007 - HM-HIM HL MH Separated Assortments, 80/AMIS – Sudanese mission

NATO Military Liaison Team in Addis Ababa – Weekly Sitrep 31/07, covering period 25 – 31 July 2007 - HM-HIM HL MH Separated Assortments, 78-I/AMIS – Sudanese mission

Offer of additional support of the European Union for the AU mission in Darfur, Sudan (AMIS II). HM-HIM HL MH Separated Assortments, 80/AMIS – Sudanese mission

Official Note: Hungarian Government and NGO support to Darfur, 08. September 2004. - HM-HIM HL MH Separated Assortments, 79/AMIS – Sudanese mission

PCS/AHG/Comm – 27.05. 2004. - HM-HIM HL MH Separated Assortments, 75/AMIS – Sudanese mission

Press Information - Javier Solana, EU High Representative for the CFSP, to meet with the Chairman of the African Union Commission Alpha Oumar Konare, Tuesday 17 May 2005 - HM-HIM HL MH Separated Assortments, 80/AMIS – Sudanese mission

PSC meeting memorandum, 06. July 2004. - HM-HIM HL MH Separated Assortments, 79/AMIS – Sudanese mission

PSC meeting.03 June 2004 - HM-HIM HL MH Separated Assortments, 80/AMIS – Sudanese mission

PSD/246/B/3121 - HM-HIM HL MH Separated Assortments, 80/ AMIS – Sudanese mission

PSD/DITF/NV/030 - HM-HIM HL MH Separated Assortments, 80/AMIS – Sudanese mission

PSD/DITF/NV/1365 - HM-HIM HL MH Separated Assortments, 80/AMIS – Sudanese mission

Report: Council Secretariat AMIS II assessment mission 16-22 September 2005 - HM-HIM HL MH Separated Assortments, 78-II/AMIS – Sudanese mission

Report: Council Secretariat AMIS II Assessment mission 16 – 22 September 2005 - HM-HIM HL MH Separated Assortments, 80/AMIS – Sudanese mission

Report on Darfur airlift, 25 October 2005. - HM-HIM HL MH Separated Assortments, 77/AMIS – Sudanese mission

Report on Darfur situation 10 March 2015. - HM-HIM HL MH Separated Assortments, 76/AMIS – Sudanese mission

SG (2005) 0446 - HM-HIM HL MH Separated Assortments, 78-I/ AMIS – Sudanese mission

SITREP as of 15 November 2004, African Mission in Sudan, Ceasefire Commission - HM-HIM HL MH Separated Assortments, 82/AMIS – Sudanese mission

SITREP as of 30 November 2004, African Mission in Sudan, Ceasefire Commission, 3. - HM-HIM HL MH Separated Assortments, 82/AMIS – Sudanese mission

SITREP as of 8 November 2004, African Mission in Sudan, Ceasefire Commission, CFC - HM-HIM HL MH Separated Assortments, 82/AMIS – Sudanese mission

Situation Report as of 25/10/04, African Mission in Sudan, Ceasefire Commission, 1. - HM-HIM HL MH Separated Assortments, 82/AMIS – Sudanese mission

Situation report on the activities of the Cease Fire Commission since June 2004, African Union, pp. 2-3. - HM-HIM HL MH Separated Assortments, 82/AMIS – Sudanese mission

Situation report on the activities of the Cease Fire Commission since June 2004, 05. October 2004. p. 2. - HM-HIM HL MH Separated Assortments, 82/AMIS – Sudanese mission

Situation report on the activities of the Cease Fire Commission since June 2004, African Union, 2. - HM-HIM HL MH Separated Assortments, 82/AMIS – Sudanese mission

Speaking Notes – EUMC-meeting 10 November 2004. - HM-HIM HL MH Separated Assortments, 75/AMIS – Sudanese mission

Status of EU Assistance Mission to AMIS II. and shortfall in personnel, Brussels, 18th August 2005 - HM-HIM HL MH Separated Assortments, 78-II/AMIS- Sudanese mission

Status of Mission Agreement (SOMA) on the establishment and management of the Ceasefire Commission in the Darfur area of the Sudan (CFC), Khartoum, 4 June 2004. - HM-HIM HL MH Separated Assortments, 82/AMIS – Sudanese mission

Strengthening EU Action in Response to Developments in Darfur, Brussels, 30 November 2005 - HM-HIM HL MH Separated Assortments, 78-II/AMIS – Sudanese mission

Summary report of Major Ferenc Kajári, 21 March 2005. - HM-HIM HL MH Separated Assortments, 75/AMIS – Sudanese mission

The AU assessment mission to Darfur Sudan 10-22 March 2005, Report of the joint assessment team - HM-HIM HL MH Separated Assortments, 77/AMIS – Sudanese mission

The AU assessment mission to Darfur Sudan 10-22 March 2005, Report of the joint assessment team, 5. - HM-HIM HL MH Separated Assortments, 77/AMIS – Sudanese mission

The AU assessment mission to Darfur Sudan 10-22 March 2005, Report of the joint assessment team, 12-13. - HM-HIM HL MH Separated Assortments, 77/AMIS – Sudanese mission

The AU assessment mission to Darfur Sudan 10-22 March 2005, Report of the joint assessment team, 13-14. - HM-HIM HL MH Separated Assortments, 77/AMIS – Sudanese mission

The AU assessment mission to Darfur Sudan 10-22 March 2005, Report of the joint assessment team, pp. 18 - 23. - HM-HIM HL MH Separated Assortments, 77/AMIS – Sudanese mission

The AU assessment mission to Darfur Sudan 10-22 March 2005, Report of the joint assessment team, 23-24. - HM-HIM HL MH Separated Assortments, 77/AMIS – Sudanese Mission

UN Security Council, *Belgium, Congo, France, Italy, Peru, Slovakia and United Kingdom of Great Britain and Northern Ireland: draft resolution S/2007/468*, 2007, https://digitallibrary.un.org/record/604362, accessed 25 March 2023

UN Security Council, *Report of the Secretary-General and the Chairperson of the African Union Commission on the hybrid operation in Darfur. S/2007/307/Rev.1.,* 2007, https://www.securitycouncilreport.org/atf/cf/%7B65BFCF9B-6D27-4E9C-8CD3-CF6E4FF96FF9%7D/Sudan%20S2007%20307%20Rev%201.pdf, accessed 09 March 2023

UN Security Council, *Report of the Security Council mission to the Sudan and Chad. S/2006/433,* 2006, https://reliefweb.int/sites/reliefweb.int/files/resources/5B2AD2B682E89B948525719B006D6832-unsc-sdn-22jun.pdf, accessed 06 March 2023

UN Security Council, *Resolution 1769 (2007) Adopted by the Security Council at its 5727th meeting on 31 July 2007.* http://unscr.com/en/resolutions/doc/1769, accessed 13 March 2023

World Bank Report, *Sudan: Stabilization and Reconstruction,* No. 24620, 2003/6/30, https://documents.worldbank.org/en/publication/documents-reports/documentdetail/440091468777571140/main-text, accessed 25 March 2023

Online Sources:

Abdul-Jalil, Musa Adam; Mohamed, Adam Azzain and Ahmed Adam Yousuf. 2007. "Future Prospects for Native Administration and Local Governance in Darfur", In *War in Darfur and the Search for Peace*, edited by de Waal, Alexander, 5-6. Cambridge, MA: Global Equity Initiative: Harvard University, https://www.academia.edu/31376523/Future_Prospects_for_Native_Administration_and_Local_Governance_in_Darfur accessed 04 February 2023

Anon., Austrian Red Cross/ACCORD, *Darfur COI Compilation*, ACCORD, https://www.ecoi.net/en/file/local/1410452/90_1506666527_accord-coi-compilation-darfur-september-2017.pdf accessed 20 January 2023

Anon., 'Besides, Darfur Destroyed: Ethnic Cleansing by Government and Militia Forces in Western Sudan', *Human Right Watch*, vol. 16, issue 6(A) (2004), https://www.hrw.org/report/2004/05/06/darfur-destroyed/ethnic-cleansing-government-and-militia-forces-western-sudan, accessed 04 February 2023

Anon., Committee on Foreign Relations United States Senate, *Darfur revisited: the international response: hearing before the Committee on Foreign Relations United States Senate. September 28, 2005.* U.S. Government Printing Office, 2007, https://www.foreign.senate.gov/imo/media/doc/092805_Transcript_Darfur%20Revisited.pdf accessed 25 March 2023

Anon., 'Darfur 2007: Chaos by Design, Peacekeeping Challenges for AMIS and UNAMID', *Human Rights Watch*, vol. 19, issue 15(A) (2007), https://www.hrw.org/report/2007/09/19/darfur-2007-chaos-design/peacekeeping-challenges-amis-and-unamid, accessed 04 February 2023

Anon., 'Darfur in Flames: Atrocities in Western Sudan', *Human Right Watch*, vol. 16, issue 5(A) (2004), https://www.hrw.org/reports/2004/sudan0404/sudan0404.pdf, accessed 04 February 2023

Anon., Darfur Joint Assessment Mission, Situation Analysis: Agriculture, Livestock and Rural Livelihoods in the Greater Darfur Region. 2012, http://www.darfurconference.com/sites/default/files/files/8%20-%20Thematic 20Working 20Group%20Agriculture%2C%20Livestock%20and%20

Rural%20
Livelihoods%20 Report (1).pdf accessed 21 January 2023

Anon., 'Darfur revisited: the international response: hearing before the Committee on Foreign Relations United States Senate', *US Government, U.S. Government Printing Office*, September 28, 2005, https://www.foreign.senate.gov/imo/media/doc/092805_Transcript_Darfur%20Revisited.pdf, accessed 20 January 2023

Anon., 'Darfur: Revitalizing the peace process', *International Crisis Group, Africa Report* issue 125 (2007), https://www.ecosonline.org/reports/2007/ICG125_darfur__revitalising_the_peace_process.pdf, accessed 09 March 2023

Anon., 'Darfur's Fragile Peace Agreement', *International Crisis Group, Policy Briefing, Africa Briefing*, issue 39 (2006), https://www.files.ethz.ch/isn/18991/b039_darfur_s_fragile_peace_agreement.pdf, accessed 06 March 2023

Anon., 'Dpko Asg Annabi Makes Transition Progress with AU', *Wikileaks, Cablegate, Scoop*, 06ADDISABABA1003, 2006, https://www.scoop.co.nz/stories/WL0604/S00138.htm, accessed 06 March 2023

Anon., 'Imperatives for Immediate Change - The African Union Mission in Sudan', *Human Rights Watch*, vol. 18, issue 1(A) (2006), https://www.hrw.org/sites/default/files/reports/sudan0106webwcover.pdf, accessed 04 February 2023

Anon., 'Sudan: Now or never in Darfur', *International Crisis Group, Africa Report*, issue 80 (2004), https://www.files.ethz.ch/isn/28762/080_sudan_now_or_never_in_darfur.pdf, accessed 04 February 2023

Anon., 'Sudan: Tripoli summit rejects foreign interference in Darfur', *reliefweb.int*, 2005, https://reliefweb.int/report/sudan/sudan-tripoli-summit-rejects-foreign-interference-darfur, accessed 13 February 2023

Besenyő, János, 'EU Support to the African Union Mission in Darfur – AMIS', *Tradecraft Review, Periodical of the Scientific Board of Military Security Office*, Special Issue (2009), http://dx.doi.org/10.2139/ssrn.3610699, accessed 25 March 2023

Besenyő, János, 'First military operation between European Union and African Union. The European Advisors role in Darfur (AMIS)', *AARMS*. vol. 6, issue 4 (2007), http://real.mtak.hu/83791/1/18bese.pdf, accessed 22 March 2023

Besenyő, János, 'Logistic Experiences: The Case of Darfur -Promoting Peace and Security in Africa', *Finnish Department of Strategic and Defence Studies*, vol. 2, issue 35 (2006), http://www.doria.fi/bitstream/handle/10024/77169/StratL2_35.pdf?sequence=1, accessed 22 March 2023

Breitkreuz, Franz; Breitkreuz, Christoph; Coyle, David A.; El Hur, Bushra; Heinrich, Wilhelm; Paulick, Holger; Pudlo, Dieter; Smith, Robyn and Steiner, Gesine, 'The alkaline Meidob volcanic field (Late Cenozoic, northwest Sudan)', *Journal of African Earth Sciences*, vol. 25, issue 2 (1997), https://www.sciencedirect.com/science/article/abs/pii/S0899536297001036, accessed 20 January 2023

Coleman, Katharina P. and Williams, Paul D., 'Logistics Partnerships in Peace Operations', *International Peace Institute*, 2017, https://www.ipinst.org/wp-content/uploads/2017/06/170615-Logistics-Partnerships.pdf, accessed 13 February 2023

Dagne, Ted, 'Sudan: Humanitarian Crisis, Peace Talks, Terrorism, and U.S. Policy', *CRS Issue Brief for Congress*, April 12, 2006, https://fas.org/sgp/crs/row/IB98043.pdf, accessed 04 February 2023

Flint, Julie, 'Sudan, Darfur Destroyed: Ethnic Cleansing by Government and Militia Forces in Western Sudan', *Human Rights Watch* (2004), https://www.hrw.org/report/2004/05/06/darfur-destroyed/ethnic-cleansing-government-and-militia-forces-western-sudan, accessed 25 March 2023

Lindsay, Tony, *Darfur – A Cultural Handbook* (Watchfield, Swindon: Defence Academy of the United Kingdom, 2007), https://www.files.ethz.ch/isn/43307/07_Apr.pdf, accessed 04 February 2023

Morton, James, 'A Darfur Compendium. A Review of the Geographical, Historical and Economic Background to the Development in the Region', *Hemel Hempstead* (2005), https://www.cmi.no/file/1852-A-Darfur-compendium.pdf, accessed 20 January 2023

Morton, James, 'Agricultural Development in Darfur Region, Sudan. Reference to Innovation, Technical Change and Open Access Resources'. *PhD thesis*, London University, March 1993, http://www.jfmorton.co.uk/pdfs/PhdBook.pdf, accessed 21 January 2023

Tubiana, Jérôme, 'Land and Power: The Case of the Zaghawa', *African Arguments*. May 28, 2008, https://africanarguments.org/2008/05/28/land-and-power-the-case-of-the-zaghawa/, accessed 20 January 2023

Tubiana, Jérôme; Tanner, Victor and Abdul-Jalil, Musa Adam, 'Traditional authorities' peacemaking role in Darfur', *United States Institute of Peace*, 2012, https://files.ethz.ch/isn/155469/PW83.pdf, accessed 20 January 2023

Monographs and Articles:

Akasha, Mohamed Osman, *Darfur: A tragedy of climate change* (Hamburg: Anchor Academic Publishing, 2004)

Ali, Hamid Eltgani (ed), *Darfur's Political Economy: A Quest for Development* (Abingdon, Oxon: Routledge, 2015)

Anyidoho, Henry Kwami, *Guns Over Kigali: The Rwandese Civil War-1994. A Personal Account* (Accra: Woeli Publishing Services, 1997)

Appiah-Mensah, Seth, 'The African Mission in Sudan: Darfur dilemmas', *African Security Studies*, vol. 15, issue 1 (2006), pp. 1–19

Besenyő, János, *Dárfúr, a lángoló tartomány, Az Afrikai Unió szudáni missziójának története* (Pécs: Publikon Kiadó, 2016)

Besenyő, János, *Darfur Peacekeepers - The African Union peacekeeping mission in darfur (AMIS) from the perspective of a Hungarian military advisor* (Paris, L'Harmattan, 2021)

Burr, Millard and Collins, Robert O., *Darfur: The Long Road to Disaster* (Princeton, NJ: Markus Wiener, 2006)

Charron, Andrea; Zyla, Benjamin and Boulden, Jane, 'NATO, the EU and Darfur: Separate but Together', in Peter Schmidt (ed.). *A Hybrid Relationship: Transatlantic Cooperation beyond NATO* (Frankfurt: a. M.: Peter Lang, 2007), pp. 147–160

Clammer, Paul, *Sudan. The Bradt Travel Guide* (Chalfont St Peter: The Bradt Travel Guides Ltd, 2005)

Copson, Raymond W., *Africa's Wars and Prospects for Peace* (Abingdon, Oxon: Routledge, 2015)

Daly, M. W., *Darfur's Sorrow: The Forgotten History of a Humanitarian Disaster* (Cambridge: Cambridge University Press, 2010)

Fadlalla, Mohamed H., *Short History of Sudan* (New York: iUniverse Inc., 2004)

Fadlalla, Mohamed H., *The Problem of Dar Fur* (New York: iUniverse Inc., 2005)

Fage, John D.; Roberts, Andrew D. and Oliver, Roland Anthony, *The Cambridge History of Africa,* Vol 7 (Cambridge: Cambridge University Press, 1986)
Fisher, William Bayne, *The Middle East: a physical, social, and regional geography* (London, New York: Methuen Dutton, 1971)
Flint, Julie and De Waal, Alex, *Darfur, A New History of a Long War* (London: Zed Books, 2005)
Gerting, Béla: *Kontinensek földrajza II.* (Budapest: Tankönyvkiadó, 1989)
Hamilton, Rebecca, *Fighting for Darfur: Public Action and the Struggle to Stop Genocide* (New York: Palgrave Macmillan, 2011)
Hastrup, Anders, *The War in Darfur: Reclaiming Sudanese History* (Abingdon, Oxon: Routledge, 2013)
Ibbotson, Sophie and Lovell-Hoare, Max, *Sudan. The Bradt Travel Guide.* 3rd edition. (Chalfont St. Peter: Bradt Travel Guides Ltd, 2012)
Kibreab, Gaim, *State Intervention and the Environment in Sudan, 1889-1989: The Demise of Communal Resource Management* (Lewiston, NY: Edvin Mellen Press, 2002)
Kramer, S. Robert; Lobban, Jr. Richard A. and Fluehr-Lobban, Carolyn, *Historical Dictionary of the Sudan.* 4th edition (Lanham, Maryland: Scarecrow Press, 2013)
Levy, Patricia and Latif, Zawia Abdul, *Sudan* (New York: Marshall Cavendish Benchmark, 2008)
Lobban, Richard A., *Historical Dictionary of Ancient and Medieval Nubia* (Lanham, Maryland: Scarecrow Press Inc, 2003)
Mahmood, Othman O., *The Root Causes of the United Nations' Failure in Somalia: The Role of Neighbouring Countries in the Somali Crisis* (Bloomington: iUniverse, 2011)
Mamdani, Mahmood, *Saviors and survivors, Darfur, Politics, and the War on Terror* (London: Verso, 2009)
Murison, Katherine (ed), *Africa South of the Sahara*, 33rd edition (London and New York: Europa Publications, 2004)
Olson, James Stuart and Shadle, Robert (eds.), *Historical Dictionary of the British Empire* (Westport, Conn.: Greenwood Press, 1996)
Pugh, Roy J. M., *Wingate Pasha: The Life of General Sir Francis Reginald Wingate, 1861–1953* (Barnsley, South Yorkshire: Pen and Sword, 2011), pp. XIII–XVI
Shillington, Kevin (ed), *Encyclopedia of African History* (New York: Fitzroy Dearborn, 2005)
Stiansen, Endre and Kevane, Michael (eds.), *Kordafan Invaded: Peripheral Incorporation and Social Transformation in Islamic Africa* (Leiden: Brill, 1998)
Suliman, Osman, *The Darfur Conflict: Geography or Institutions?* (New York: Routledge, 2011)
Svenson, Emma, *The African mission in Burundi, Lessons Learned from the African Union's first peace operation,* FOI-R-2561-SE. Stockholm, 2008

NOTES

Chapter 1

1 Mohamed H. Fadlalla, *Short History of Sudan* (New York: iUniverse Inc., 2004), p. 57.
2 Gaim Kibreab, *State Intervention and the Environment in Sudan, 1889-1989: The Demise of Communal Resource Management* (Lewiston, NY: Edvin Mellen Press, 2002), pp. 86, 93–98, 123.
3 Béla Gerting, *Kontinensek földrajza II* (Budapest: Tankönyvkiadó, 1989), pp. 85–86.
4 Franz Breitkreuz, et al., 'The alkaline Meidob volcanic field (Late Cenozoic, northwest Sudan)', *Journal of African Earth Sciences*, vol. 25, issue 2 (1997), https://www.sciencedirect.com/science/article/abs/pii/S0899536297001036, accessed 20 January 2023, pp. 1–2.; James Morton, 'A Darfur Compendium. A Review of the Geographical, Historical and Economic Background to the Development in the Region', *Hemel Hempstead* (2005), https://www.cmi.no/file/1852-A-Darfur-compendium.pdf, accessed 20 January 2023, p. 3.
5 Katherine Murison (ed), *Africa South of the Sahara*, 33rd edition. (London and New York: Europa Publications, 2004), p. 1,060.
6 Paul Clammer, *Sudan. The Bradt Travel Guide* (Chalfont St Peter: The Bradt Travel Guides Ltd, 2005), p. 5.
7 Anon., Darfur Joint Assessment Mission, Situation Analysis: Agriculture, Livestock and Rural Livelihoods in the Greater Darfur Region. 2012, http://www.darfurconference.com/sites/default/files/files/8%20-%20Thematic 20Working 20Group%20Agriculture%2C%20Livestock%20and%20 Rural%20Livelihoods%20 Report (1).pdf accessed 21 January 2023.; Morton (2005), p. 3.; James Morton, 'Agricultural Development in Darfur Region, Sudan. Reference to Innovation, Technical Change and Open Access Resources'. *PhD thesis*, London University, March 1993, http://www.jfmorton.co.uk/pdfs/PhdBook.pdf, accessed 21 January 2023, p. 2.; Hamid Eltgani Ali (ed), *Darfur's Political Economy: A Quest for Development* (Abingdon, Oxon: Routledge, 2015), pp. 69–70.
8 Patricia Levy and Zawia Abdul Latif, *Sudan* (New York: Marshall Cavendish Benchmark, 2008), p. 17.
9 William Bayne Fisher, *The Middle East: a physical, social, and regional geography* (London, New York: Methuen Dutton, 1971), p. 576.
10 Raymond W. Copson, *Africa's Wars and Prospects for Peace* (Abingdon, Oxon: Routledge, 2015), p. 29.
11 Fisher, pp. 582–583.; World Bank Report, *Sudan: Stabilization and Reconstruction,* No. 24620, 2003/6/30, https://documents.worldbank.org/en/publication/documents-reports/documentdetail/440091468777571140/main-text, accessed 25 March 2023, p. 89.
12 Fisher, pp. 230–231.
13 Mohamed H. Fadlalla, *The Problem of Dar Fur* (New York: iUniverse Inc., 2005), pp. 23–28.; Clammer, pp. 214–215.
14 Committee on Foreign Relations United States Senate, *Darfur revisited: the international response: hearing before the Committee on Foreign Relations United States Senate. September 28, 2005.* U.S. Government Printing Office, 2007, https://www.foreign.senate.gov/imo/media/doc/092805_Transcript_Darfur%20Revisited.pdf, accessed 04 February 2023; Anon., Austrian Red Cross/ACCORD, *Darfur COI Compilation*, ACCORD, https://www.ecoi.net/en/file/local/1410452/90_1506666527_accord-coi-compilation-darfur-september-2017.pdf, accessed 20 January 2023.
15 Rebecca Hamilton, *Fighting for Darfur: Public Action and the Struggle to Stop Genocide* (New York: Palgrave Macmillan, 2011), pp. 13–16; M. W. Daly, *Darfur's Sorrow: The Forgotten History of a Humanitarian Disaster* (Cambridge: Cambridge University Press, 2010), pp. 15–38; Jérôme Tubiana, Victor Tanner, and Musa Adam Abdul-Jalil, 'Traditional authorities' peacemaking role in Darfur', *United States Institute of Peace*, 2012, https://files.ethz.ch/isn/155469/PW83.pdf, accessed 20 January 2023.
16 János Besenyő, *Dárfúr, a lángoló tartomány, Az Afrikai Unió szudáni missziójának története* (Pécs: Publikon Kiadó, 2016), p. 18.; Anon. (2017).
17 Jérôme Tubiana, 'Land and Power: The Case of the Zaghawa', *African Arguments*, May 28, 2008, https://africanarguments.org/2008/05/28/land-and-power-the-case-of-the-zaghawa/, accessed 20 January 2023.; Anon. (2017).
18 Julie Flint and Alex De Waal, *Darfur, A New History of a Long War* (London: Zed Books, 2005), p. 77.
19 Morton, p. 4.; Tony Lindsay, *Darfur – A Cultural Handbook* (Watchfield, Swindon: Defence Academy of the United Kingdom, 2007), https://www.files.ethz.ch/isn/43307/07_Apr.pdf, accessed 04 February 2023.; Richard

A. Lobban, *Historical Dictionary of Ancient and Medieval Nubia* (Lanham, Maryland: Scarecrow Press Inc, 2003), pp. 129.

20 Mahmood Mamdani, *Saviors and survivors, Darfur, Politics, and the War on Terror* (London: Verso, 2009), pp. 89, 134.

21 Morton (2005), pp. 22.; Mohamed Osman Akasha, *Darfur: A tragedy of climate change* (Hamburg: Anchor Academic Publishing, 2004), p. 30.; Osman Suliman, *The Darfur Conflict: Geography or Institutions?* (New York: Routledge, 2011), p. 2.

22 Mamdani, p. 134.; Morton (2005), p. 23.

23 Sophie Ibbotson and Max Lovell-Hoare, *Sudan. The Bradt Travel Guide.* 3rd edition. (Chalfont St. Peter: Bradt Travel Guides Ltd, 2012), p. 214.

24 S. Robert Kramer, Richard A. Lobban, Jr. and Carolyn Fluehr-Lobban, *Historical Dictionary of the Sudan.* 4th edition (Lanham, Maryland: Scarecrow Press, 2013), p. 120.; Endre Stiansen, and Michael Kevane (eds.), *Kordafan Invaded: Peripheral Incorporation and Social Transformation in Islamic Africa* (Leiden: Brill, 1998), pp. 52–55.

25 Eltgani, p. 11.

26 Lindsay (2007).

27 Rudolf Anton Carl Freiherr von Slatin (1857–1932): colonial official and soldier. For more on him see Roy J. M. Pugh, *Wingate Pasha: The Life of General Sir Francis Reginald Wingate, 1861–1953* (Barnsley, South Yorkshire: Pen and Sword, 2011), pp. XIII–XVI.

28 Kramer, Lobban and Fluehr-Lobban, p. 120.; Eltgani, pp.12–13.; Akasha, pp. 30–31.; Anders Hastrup, *The War in Darfur: Reclaiming Sudanese History* (Abingdon, Oxon: Routledge, 2013), pp. 30–33.

29 Clammer, p. 31.; John D. Fage, Andrew D. Roberts, and Roland Anthony Oliver, *The Cambridge History of Africa,* Vol 7. (Cambridge: Cambridge University Press, 1986), p. 762.; Eltgani, p. 13.

30 James Stuart Olson and Robert Shadle, (eds.), *Historical Dictionary of the British Empire* (Westport, Conn.: Greenwood Press, 1996), p. 53.; Kevin Shillington (ed), *Encyclopedia of African History* (New York: Fitzroy Dearborn, 2005), p. 803.

31 Musa Adam Abdul-Jalil, Adam Azzain Mohamed, and Ahmed Adam Yousuf, "Future Prospects for Native Administration and Local Governance in Darfur", In *War in Darfur and the Search for Peace*, edited by de Waal, Alexander (Cambridge, MA: Global Equity Initiative: Harvard University, 2007), pp. 5–6; https://www.academia.edu/31376523/Future_Prospects_for_Native_Administration_and_Local_Governance_in_Darfur, accessed 04 February 2023.; Murison, p. 1,061.

32 Julie Flint, 'Sudan, Darfur Destroyed: Ethnic Cleansing by Government and Militia Forces in Western Sudan', *Human Rights Watch* (2004), https://www.hrw.org/report/2004/05/06/darfur-destroyed/ethnic-cleansing-government-and-militia-forces-western-sudan, accessed 25 March 2023.

33 Millard Burr and Robert O. Collins, *Darfur: The Long Road to Disaster* (Princeton, NJ: Markus Wiener, 2006), p. 287.

Chapter 2

1 Anon., 'Darfur in Flames: Atrocities in Western Sudan', *Human Right Watch*, vol. 16, issue 5(A) (2004), https://www.hrw.org/reports/2004/sudan0404/sudan0404.pdf, accessed 04 February 2023.; Anon., 'Besides, Darfur Destroyed: Ethnic Cleansing by Government and Militia Forces in Western Sudan', *Human Right Watch*, vol. 16, issue 6(A) (2004), https://www.hrw.org/report/2004/05/06/darfur-destroyed/ethnic-cleansing-government-and-militia-forces-western-sudan, accessed 04 February 2023.

2 Hastrup, pp. 78–99.

3 Anon. (2004).

4 János Besenyő, 'Logistic Experiences: The Case of Darfur – Promoting Peace and Security in Africa', *Finnish Department of Strategic and Defence Studies*, vol. 2, issue 35 (2006), http://www.doria.fi/bitstream/handle/10024/77169/StratL2_35.pdf?sequence=1, accessed 22 March 2023.

5 Fact Sheet: EU Response to the crisis in Darfur, Brussels, 10th June 2004 - HM-HIM HL MH Separated Assortments, 78-II/AMIS – Sudanese mission.

6 Anon., 'Sudan: Now or never in Darfur', *International Crisis Group, Africa Report*, issue 80 (2004), https://www.files.ethz.ch/isn/28762/080_sudan_now_or_never_in_darfur.pdf, accessed 04 February 2023.

7 Ted Dagne, 'Sudan: Humanitarian Crisis, Peace Talks, Terrorism, and U.S. Policy', *CRS Issue Brief for Congress*, April 12, 2006, https://fas.org/sgp/crs/row/IB98043.pdf, accessed 04 February 2023.

8 African Union, *The African Union and the conflict in the Darfur region of the Sudan. Meeting the challenges of peace, security and stability, CONF/PLG/3(I),* Addis Ababa, 2005, https://reliefweb.int/sites/reliefweb.int/files/resources/A0AD919C2B396D0FC125700D004A49AC-au-afr-26may.pdf accessed 04 February 2023.

9 Anon., 'Imperatives for Immediate Change - The African Union Mission in Sudan', *Human Rights Watch*, vol. 18, issue 1(A) (2006), https://www.hrw.org/sites/default/files/reports/sudan0106webwcover.pdf, accessed 04 February 2023.

10 Katharina P Coleman, and Paul D. Williams, 'Logistics Partnerships in Peace Operations', *International Peace Institute*, 2017, https://www.ipinst.org/wp-content/uploads/2017/06/170615-Logistics-Partnerships.pdf, accessed 13 February 2023

11 African Union, *Agreement with the Sudanese Parties on the Modalities for the Establishment of the Ceasefire Commission and the Deployment of Observers in the Darfur,* Addis Ababa, 2004, https://peacemaker.un.org/sudan-darfur-ceasefire-commission2004 accessed 04 February 2023.

12 Situation report on the activities of the Cease Fire Commission since June 2004, African Union, pp. 2–3. - HM-HIM HL MH Separated Assortments, 82/AMIS – Sudanese mission.

13 Situation report on the activities of the Cease Fire Commission since June 2004, 05. October 2004. p. 2. - HM-HIM HL MH Separated Assortments, 82/AMIS – Sudanese mission.

14 Status of Mission Agreement (SOMA) on the establishment and management of the Ceasefire Commission in the Darfur area of the Sudan (CFC), Khartoum, 4 June 2004. - HM-HIM HL MH Separated Assortments, 82/AMIS – Sudanese mission

15 Anon., (2006).

16 Anon. (2007).; The AU assessment mission to Darfur Sudan 10-22 March 2005, Report of the joint assessment team, 5. - HM-HIM HL MH Separated Assortments, 77/AMIS – Sudanese mission.

17 Meeting Note Sudan/Darfur, 28 June 2004, 1. - HM-HIM HL MH Separated Assortments, 82/AMIS – Sudanese mission.

18 For more on this theme see: Othman O. Mahmood, *The Root Causes of the United Nations' Failure in Somalia: The Role of Neighbouring Countries in the Somali Crisis* (Bloomington: iUniverse, 2011), pp. 52–56.

19 Situation Report as of 25/10/04, African Mission in Sudan, Ceasefire Commission, 1. - HM-HIM HL MH Separated Assortments, 82/AMIS – Sudanese mission.

20 Anon., 'Darfur 2007: Chaos by Design, Peacekeeping Challenges for AMIS and UNAMID', *Human Rights Watch*, vol. 19, issue 15(A) (2007), https://www.hrw.org/report/2007/09/19/darfur-2007-chaos-design/peacekeeping-challenges-amis-and-unamid, accessed 04 February 2023.

21 Summary report of Major Ferenc Kajári, 21 March 2005.- HM-HIM HL MH Separated Assortments, 75/AMIS – Sudanese mission; Speaking Notes – EUMC-meeting 10 November 2004. - HM-HIM HL MH Separated Assortments, 75/AMIS – Sudanese mission and Interview with members of AMIS II mission, who insisted on their anonymity.

22 Report on Darfur situation 10 March 2015.- HM-HIM HL MH Separated Assortments, 76/AMIS – Sudanese mission.

23 IM 07-07/03 DG 193/06 - HM-HIM HL MH Separated Assortments, 78-II/AMIS – Sudanese mission.

Chapter 3

1 African Union, *Briefing Note on the renewal of the mandate of the AU Mission in the Sudan (AMIS) - PSC/PR/2 (XLII),* Addis Ababa, 2005, http://www.peaceau.org/uploads/reportmandateeng.pdf, accessed 13 February 2023.

2 African Union, *The African Union...* (2005).

3 The AU assessment mission to Darfur Sudan 10-22 March 2005, Report of the joint assessment team - HM-HIM HL MH Separated Assortments, 77/AMIS – Sudanese mission.

4 EU Organisation Arrangements to Manage the Consolidated Package of Support to AMIS II - HM-HIM HL MH Separated Assortments, 78-I/AMIS – Sudanese mission.

5 SITREP as of 8 November 2004, African Mission in Sudan, Ceasefire Commission, CFC - HM-HIM HL MH Separated Assortments, 82/AMIS – Sudanese mission.

6 SITREP as of 30 November 2004, African Mission in Sudan, Ceasefire Commission, 3. - HM-HIM HL MH Separated Assortments, 82/AMIS – Sudanese mission.

7 HM-HIM HL MH Separated Assortments, 78-II/AMIS - Sudanese mission.

8 SITREP as of 15 November 2004, African Mission in Sudan, Ceasefire Commission - HM-HIM HL MH Separated Assortments, 82/AMIS – Sudanese mission.

9 SITREP as of 30 November 2004, African Mission in Sudan, Ceasefire Commission, 2. - HM-HIM HL MH Separated Assortments, 82/AMIS – Sudanese mission.
10 African Union, *Briefing Note*... (2005).
11 Information paper on Sudan/Darfur and AMIS EUMC 2 February 2005 - HM-HIM HL MH Separated Assortments, 78-I/AMIS – Sudanese mission.
12 HM-HIM HL MH Separated Assortments, 77/AMIS – Sudanese mission.
13 The AU assessment mission to Darfur Sudan 10-22 March 2005, Report of the joint assessment team, pp. 12–13. - HM-HIM HL MH Separated Assortments, 77/AMIS – Sudanese mission.
14 The AU assessment mission to Darfur Sudan 10-22 March 2005, Report of the joint assessment team, pp. 13–14. - HM-HIM HL MH Separated Assortments, 77/AMIS – Sudanese mission.
15 The AU assessment mission to Darfur Sudan 10-22 March 2005, Report of the joint assessment team, pp. 18– 23. - HM-HIM HL MH Separated Assortments, 77/AMIS – Sudanese mission.
16 The AU assessment mission to Darfur Sudan 10-22 March 2005, Report of the joint assessment team, pp. 23–24. - HM-HIM HL MH Separated Assortments, 77/AMIS – Sudanese Mission.
17 African Union, *The African Union and the conflict in the Darfur region of the Sudan. Meeting the challenges of peace, security and stability, CONF/PLG/3(I).* Addis Ababa, 2005, https://reliefweb.int/sites/reliefweb.int/files/resources/A0AD919C2B396D0FC125700D004A49AC-au-afr-26may.pdf accessed 13 February 2023.
18 Pan African News Agency, *Sudan: Tripoli summit rejects foreign interference in Darfur,* 2005, https://m.reliefweb.int/report/173977/sudan/sudan-tripoli-summit-rejects-foreign-interference-darfur accessed 13 February 2023.
19 African Union, *Briefing Note on the renewal of the mandate of the AU Mission in the Sudan (AMIS) - PSC/PR/2 (XLII),* Addis Ababa, 2005, http://www.peaceau.org/uploads/reportmandateeng.pdf accessed 13 February 2023.; Coleman and Williams (2017).

Chapter 4

1 African Union, *Briefing Note*... (2005).; Report: Council Secretariat AMIS II Assessment mission 16 – 22 September 2005 - HM-HIM HL MH Separated Assortments, 80/AMIS – Sudanese mission; AMIS III. background, organisation - HM-HIM HL MH Separated Assortments, 80/AMIS – Sudanese mission.
2 IM 07-07/03 DG 022/06 - HM-HIM HL MH Separated Assortments, 80/AMIS – Sudanese mission.
3 IM 07-07/03 CCM 012/06 - HM-HIM HL MH Separated Assortments, 80/AMIS – Sudanese mission.
4 Report: Council Secretariat AMIS II assessment mission 16-22 September 2005 - HM-HIM HL MH Separated Assortments, 78-II/AMIS – Sudanese mission.
5 Colonel János Besenyő's unpublished diary of Darfur, p. 85.
6 African Union Darfur Integrated Task Force, Weekly Report No. 16., 16. August to 12 September 2005, 9. - HM-HIM HL MH Separated Assortments, 77/AMIS – Sudanese mission.
7 African Union Darfur Integrated Task Force, Weekly Report No. 16., 16. August to 12 September 2005, 6-7. - HM-HIM HL MH Separated Assortments, 77/AMIS – Sudanese mission.
8 Interview with a member of Darfur Integrated Task Force, who insisted on his anonymity.
9 HM-HIM HL MH Separated Assortments, 77/AMIS – Sudanese mission; EU weekly report, Monday 26-Feb-07 until Sunday 04-Mar-07 - HM-HIM HL MH Separated Assortments, 77/AMIS – Sudanese mission.
10 African Union, *Briefing Note*... (2005)
11 IM 07-07/03 DG 272/06 - HM-HIM HL MH Separated Assortments, 78-II/AMIS – Sudanese mission.
12 AU Led Joint Assessment Report, 20 December 2005. - HM-HIM HL MH Separated Assortments, 78-I/AMIS – Sudanese mission.
13 AU Led Joint Assessment Report, 20 December 2005. - HM-HIM HL MH Separated Assortments, 78-I/AMIS – Sudanese mission.
14 AU Led Joint Assessment Report, 20 December 2005. - HM-HIM HL MH Separated Assortments, 78-I/AMIS – Sudanese mission.; Besenyő (2016), pp. 62–63.
15 AU Led Joint Assessment Report, 20 December 2005. - HM-HIM HL MH Separated Assortments, 78-I/AMIS – Sudanese mission.
16 János Besenyő, *Darfur Peacekeepers - The African Union peacekeeping mission in darfur (AMIS) from the perspective of a Hungarian military advisor* (Paris, L'Harmattan, 2021) p. 86.
17 Strengthening EU Action in Response to Developments in Darfur, Brussels, 30 November 2005 - HM-HIM HL MH Separated Assortments, 78-II/AMIS – Sudanese mission.
18 Briefing by Dr. Salim Ahmed Salim, AU Special Envoy and Chief Mediator for the Darfur Conflict, to the U.N. Security Council on 13 January 2006. Speech presented at the UN Security Council. - HM-HIM HL MH Separated Assortments, 78-II/AMIS – Sudanese mission.
19 African Union, *Communique of the 46th. meeting of the Peace and Security Council - PSC/PR/Comm. (XLV)*, Addis Ababa, Ethiopia, 2006, https://reliefweb.int/report/sudan/sudan-peace-and-security-council-46th-meeting-communique, accessed 27 February 2023
20 IM 07-07/07 CCM 079/06 - HM-HIM HL MH Separated Assortments, 78-II/AMIS – Sudanese mission.
21 The PAE executives said the 126 days would have been just enough to make it operational, the mission and the compilation of new camps, which, however, would only be able to meet the most basic needs, and do not reach the minimum requirements set by the UN. This meant that when the Organisation took over the camps, newer developments with significant costs, investments had to be made in all camps. *Colonel János Besenyő's unpublished diary of Darfur.* (Darfur: 2005), p. 98.
22 IM 07-07/07 CCM 083/06 - HM-HIM HL MH Separated Assortments, 78-II/AMIS – Sudanese mission.
23 Andrea Charron, Benjamin Zyla, and Jane Boulden, 'NATO, the EU and Darfur: Separate but Together', in Peter Schmidt (ed.). *A Hybrid Relationship: Transatlantic Cooperation beyond NATO* (Frankfurt: a. M.: Peter Lang, 2007), pp. 147–160.
24 Interview with an EU adviser, who served at Darfur in this time and who insisted on his anonymity.
25 African Union, *Report of the chairperson of the commission on the status of the implementation of the Peace and Security Council decision of 10 March 2006 on the situation in Darfur and the conclusion of the Abuja Peace Talks. PSC/MIN/2 (LI)*, Addis Ababa, 2006, https://reliefweb.int/sites/reliefweb.int/files/resources/26CC3D0F09E665B085257171007003F2-au-sdn-15may.pdf accessed 06 March 2023.
26 IM 07-07/03 CCM 077/06 - HM-HIM HL MH Separated Assortments, 78-II/AMIS – Sudanese mission.
27 Monthly Report EUSR Sudan - May 2006 - HM-HIM HL MH Separated Assortments, 78-II/AMIS – Sudanese mission.
28 IM 07-07/03 DG 368/06 - HM-HIM HL MH Separated Assortments, 78-II/AMIS – Sudanese mission.
29 Anon., 'Dpko Asg Annabi Makes Transition Progress with AU', *Wikileaks, Cablegate, Scoop*, 06ADDISABABA1003, 2006, https://www.scoop.co.nz/stories/WL0604/S00138.htm, accessed 06 March 2023.; Anon., 'Darfur's Fragile Peace Agreement', *International Crisis Group, Policy Briefing, Africa Briefing*, issue 39 (2006), https://www.files.ethz.ch/isn/18991/b039_darfur_s_fragile_peace_agreement.pdf, accessed 06 March 2023.
30 IM 07-07/03 DG 348/06 - HM-HIM HL MH Separated Assortments, 80/AMIS – Sudanese mission.
31 EUSR MA weekly report – Week 27/2007 - HM-HIM HL MH Separated Assortments, 78-II/AMIS – Sudanese mission.
32 IM 07-07/03 DG 314/06 - HM-HIM HL MH Separated Assortments, 80/AMIS – Sudanese mission.
33 IM 07-07/07 CCM 083/06 - HM-HIM HL MH Separated Assortments, 78-II/AMIS – Sudanese mission.
34 Details on the delegation and the submitted opinion: UN Security Council, *Report of the Security Council mission to the Sudan and Chad. S/2006/433,* 2006, https://reliefweb.int/report/chad/report-security-council-mission-sudan-and-chad-4-10-jun-2006-s2006433, accessed 06 March 2023.
35 Details on the delegation and the submitted opinion: UN Security Council, *Report of the Security Council mission to the Sudan and Chad. S/2006/433,* 2006, https://reliefweb.int/report/chad/report-security-council-mission-sudan-and-chad-4-10-jun-2006-s2006433, accessed 06 March 2023.
36 Details on the delegation and the submitted opinion: UN Security Council, *Report of the Security Council mission to the Sudan and Chad. S/2006/433,* 2006, https://reliefweb.int/report/chad/report-security-council-mission-sudan-and-chad-4-10-jun-2006-s2006433, accessed 06 March 2023.
37 Broad options for NATO support to the UN mission in Darfur - HM-HIM HL MH Separated Assortments, 78-I/AMIS – Sudanese mission; Coleman and Williams (2017).
38 EUSR MA weekly report – Week 06/2007 - HM-HIM HL MH Separated Assortments, 78-II/AMIS – Sudanese mission.
39 EUSR MA weekly report – Week 05/2007 - HM-HIM HL MH Separated Assortments, 78-II/AMIS – Sudanese mission.

40 EUSR MA weekly report – Week 10/2007 - HM-HIM HL MH Separated Assortments, 78-II/AMIS – Sudanese mission; Anon., 'Darfur: Revitalizing the peace process', *International Crisis Group, Africa Report* issue 125 (2007), https://www.ecosonline.org/reports/2007/ICG125_darfur__revitalising_the_peace_process.pdf, accessed 09 March 2023.
41 EUSR MA weekly report – Week 14/2007 - HM-HIM HL MH Separated Assortments, 78-II/AMIS – Sudanese mission.
42 NATO Military Liaison Team in Addis Ababa – Weekly Sitrep 16/07, covering period 12 - 20 April 2007 - HM-HIM HL MH Separated Assortments, 80/AMIS – Sudanese mission.
43 EUSR MA weekly report – Week 17/2007 - HM-HIM HL MH Separated Assortments, 78-II/AMIS – Sudanese mission.
44 EUSR MA weekly report – Week 16/2007 - HM-HIM HL MH Separated Assortments, 78-II/AMIS – Sudanese mission.
45 UN Security Council, *Report of the Secretary-General and the Chairperson of the African Union Commission on the hybrid operation in Darfur. S/2007/307/Rev.1.*, 2007, https://www.securitycouncilreport.org/atf/cf/%7B65BFCF9B-6D27-4E9C-8CD3-CF6E4FF96FF9%7D/Sudan%20S2007%20307%20Rev%201.pdf accessed 09 March 2023.
46 3000/COMJCL/023/07 - HM-HIM HL MH Separated Assortments, 80/AMIS – Sudanese mission.
47 EUSR MA weekly report – Week 15/2007 - HM-HIM HL MH Separated Assortments, 78-II/AMIS – Sudanese mission.
48 EUSR MA weekly report – Week 21/2007 - HM-HIM HL MH Separated Assortments, 78-II/AMIS – Sudanese mission.
49 EU weekly report, Monday 28-May-07 until Sunday 03- Jun-07 - HM-HIM HL MH Separated Assortments, 78-II/AMIS – Sudanese mission.
50 EUSR MA weekly report – Week 19/2007 - HM-HIM HL MH Separated Assortments, 78-II/AMIS – Sudanese mission.
51 EUSR MA weekly report – Week 25/2007 - HM-HIM HL MH Separated Assortments, 78-II/AMIS – Sudanese mission.
52 EUSR MA weekly report – Week 27/2007 - HM-HIM HL MH Separated Assortments, 78-II/AMIS – Sudanese mission.
53 EUSR MA weekly report – Week 29/2007 - HM-HIM HL MH Separated Assortments, 78-II/AMIS – Sudanese mission.
54 HSP Joint Military Strategic Concept and HSP Police CONOPS.
55 NATO Military Liaison Team in Addis Ababa – Weekly Sitrep 31/07, covering period 25 – 31 July 2007 - HM-HIM HL MH Separated Assortments, 78-I/AMIS – Sudanese mission.
56 EUSR MA weekly report – Week 16/2007 - HM-HIM HL MH Separated Assortments, 78-II/AMIS – Sudanese mission.
57 UN Security Council, *Resolution 1769 (2007) Adopted by the Security Council at its 5727th meeting on 31 July 2007.* http://unscr.com/en/resolutions/doc/1769 accessed 13 March 2023.
58 Interview with an EU adviser, who served at Darfur in this time and who insisted on his anonymity.

Chapter 5

1 EU Organisation Arrangements to Manage the Consolidated Package of Support to AMIS II- HM-HIM HL MH Separated Assortments, 78-I/AMIS – Sudanese mission.
2 Fact Sheet: EU Response to the crisis in Darfur, Brussels, 10th June 2004 - HM-HIM HL MH Separated Assortments, 78-II/AMIS – Sudanese mission.
3 PSC meeting 03 June 2004 - HM-HIM HL MH Separated Assortments, 80/AMIS – Sudanese mission.
4 EU meeting of AMIS deployed EU MILOBs and technical planning experts, IM 07-07/03 DG 188/05 - HM-HIM HL MH Separated Assortments, 80/AMIS – Sudanese mission.
5 Meeting Note Sudan/Darfur, 2004. June 28, 1. - HM-HIM HL MH Separated Assortments, 77/AMIS – Sudanese mission.
6 Situation report on the activities of the Cease Fire Commission since June 2004, African Union, 2. - HM-HIM HL MH Separated Assortments, 82/AMIS – Sudanese mission.
7 CCD 07-00/03 OPS 195/04 HM-HIM HL MH Separated Assortments, 78-I/AMIS – Sudanese mission.
8 Military Advice on the draft Action Plan for ESDP support to Peace and Security in Africa, Brussels, 2 September 2004 - HM-HIM HL MH Separated Assortments, 78-II/AMIS – Sudanese mission.
9 Draft Council Conclusions – Sudan/Darfur, Brussels, 27 October 2004 - HM-HIM HL MH Separated Assortments, 78-II/AMIS – Sudanese mission.
10 Council of the European Union. 2004. Action Plan for ESDP support to Peace and Security in Africa 10538/4/04. REV. 4. Brussels, 16. November 2004, https://data.consilium.europa.eu/doc/document/ST%2010538%202004%20REV%204/EN/pdf accessed 13 March 2023.
11 Information Paper on possible EU military implications in the light of the Action Plan for ESDP support to Peace and Security in Africa, IM 01-16/20-07 OPS 212/04 - HM-HIM HL MH Separated Assortments, 78-II/AMIS – Sudanese mission.
12 Press Information - Javier Solana, EU High Representative for the CFSP, to meet with the Chairman of the African Union Commission Alpha Oumar Konare, Tuesday 17 May 2005 - HM-HIM HL MH Separated Assortments, 80/AMIS – Sudanese mission.
13 IM 07-07/03 DG 362/06 - HM-HIM HL MH Separated Assortments, 80/AMIS – Sudanese mission.
14 NATO Military Liaison Team in Addis Ababa – Weekly Sitrep 16/07, covering period 12 – 20 April 2007 - HM-HIM HL MH Separated Assortments, 80/AMIS – Sudanese mission.
15 Information Note to the Political and Security Committee (PSC) on the Requirement to Amend the 3rd Contribution Agreement with the African Union (AU) on the Financing of the AMIS Operation in Darfur from the African Peace Facility (APF); PSD/DITF/NV/1365 - HM-HIM HL MH Separated Assortments, 80/AMIS – Sudanese mission.
16 SG (2005) 0446 - HM-HIM HL MH Separated Assortments, 78-I/AMIS – Sudanese mission.
17 IM 07-07/07 OPS 112/05 - HM-HIM HL MH Separated Assortments, 78-I/AMIS – Sudanese mission.
18 IM 07-07/03 DG 296/06 - HM-HIM HL MH Separated Assortments, 80/AMIS – Sudanese mission.
19 The USA, the UN, France, Canada, Great Britain and the Netherlands were cooperating. Besenyő (2021), pp. 123–124.
20 PSD/246/B/3121 - HM-HIM HL MH Separated Assortments, 80/AMIS – Sudanese mission.
21 Information paper on Sudan/Darfur and AMIS EUMC 2 February 2005 - HM-HIM HL MH Separated Assortments, 78-I/AMIS – Sudanese mission.
22 German/French non-paper, Sudan/Darfur: Proposals for an enhanced role of the European Union - HM-HIM HL MH Separated Assortments, 78-II/AMIS – Sudanese mission.
23 Offer of additional support of the European Union for the AU mission in Darfur, Sudan (AMIS II). HM-HIM HL MH Separated Assortments, 80/AMIS – Sudanese mission.
24 Darfur - EU Support to AMIS, DG 205/05 - HM-HIM HL MH Separated Assortments, 80/AMIS – Sudanese mission.
25 Press Information - Javier Solana, EU High Representative for the CFSP, to meet with the Chairman of the African Union Commission Alpha Oumar Konare, Tuesday 17 May 2005 - HM-HIM HL MH Separated Assortments, 80/AMIS – Sudanese mission.
26 IM 07-07/08 OPS 098/05- HM-HIM HL MH Separated Assortments, 78-I/AMIS – Sudanese mission.
27 EU Organization Arrangements to Manage the Consolidated Package of Support to AMIS II - HM-HIM HL MH Special Collection Documents, 80/AMIS - Sudanese mission.
28 Besenyő (2016), pp. 94–95.
29 Draft Concept for EU Civilian/Military Supporting Action to AMIS II - HM-HIM HL MH Separated Assortments, 78-I/AMIS – Sudanese mission.
30 IM 07-07/03 CCM 027/06 - HM-HIM HL MH Separated Assortments, 78-II/AMIS – Sudanese mission.
31 EU meeting of AMIS deployed EU MILOBs and technical planning experts, IM 07-07/03 DG 188/05 - HM-HIM HL MH Separated Assortments, 80/AMIS – Sudanese mission.
32 Council Joint Action on the European Union civilian military supporting action to the African Union mission. In the Darfur Region of Sudan – HM-HIM HLMH Separated Assortments, 77/AMIS-Sudanese mission.
33 Council Joint Action appointing a Special Representative of the European Union for Sudan, Brussels, 13 July 2005 – HM-HIM HL MH Separated Assortments, 78-II/AMIS – Sudanese mission; Javier Solana welcomes today's appointment of Pekka Haavisto as EU Special Representative for Sudan, Brussels, 18 July 2005 – HM-HIM HL MH Separated Assortments, 78-II/AMIS – Sudanese mission.
34 IM 07-07/04 DG 317/05, Brussels, 22 July 2005 – HM-HIM HL MH Separated Assortments, 78-II/AMIS- Sudanese mission.
35 EU Organisation Arrangements to Manage the Consolidated Package of Support to AMIS II. – HM-HIM HL MH Separated Assortments, 78-I/AMIS – Sudanese mission.

36 EU Organisation Arrangements to Manage the Consolidated Package of Support to AMIS II. – HM-HIM HL MH Separated Assortments, 78-I/AMIS – Sudanese mission.
37 Draft Concept for EU Civilian/Military Supporting Action to AMIS II. – HM-HIM HL MH Separated Assortments, 78-I/AMIS – Sudanese mission.
38 Status of EU Assistance Mission to AMIS II. and shortfall in personnel, Brussels, 18th August 2005 – HM-HIM HL MH Separated Assortments, 78-II/AMIS- Sudanese mission.
39 Report: Council Secretariat AMIS II assessment mission 16-22 September 2005 – HM-HIM HL MH Separated Assortments, 78-II/AMIS – Sudanese mission.
40 IM 07-07/03 CCM 046/06 – HM – HIM HL MH Separated Assortments, 78 – II/AMIS- Sudanese mission and interview with some EU advisers and military observers, who insist on their anonymity.
41 Monthly Report EUSR Sudan – April 2006 – HM-HIM HL MH Separated Assortments, 78 – II/AMIS - Sudanese mission.
42 Strengthening EU Action in Response to Developments in Darfur, Brussels, 30 November 2005 – HM – HIM HL MH Separated Assortments, 78 – II/AMIS-Sudanese mission.
43 IM 07 – 07/03 DG 498/05 – HM – HIM HL MH Separated Assortments 78-II/AMIS - Sudanese mission.
44 IM 07 – 07/03 DG 496/05 – HM – HIM HL MH Separated Assortments 78-II/AMIS - Sudanese mission.
45 IM 07 – 07/03 DG 510/05 – HM – HIM HL MH Separated Assortments 78-II/AMIS - Sudanese mission.
46 IM 07 – 07/03 DG 082/06 – HM – HIM HL MH Separated Assortments 78-II/AMIS – Sudanese mission.
47 IM 07 – 07/03 DG 365/06 – HM – HIM HL MH Separated Assortments 78-II/AMIS – Sudanese mission.
48 IM 07 – 07/07 CCM 024/06 – HM – HIM HL MH Separated Assortments 78-II/AMIS – Sudanese mission.
49 IM 07 – 07/03 DG 208/06 – HM – HIM HL MH Separated Assortments 80/AMIS – Sudanese mission.
50 IM 07 – 07/03 DG 101/06 – HM – HIM HL MH Separated Assortments 80/AMIS – Sudanese mission.
51 Besenyő (2016), p. 105.
52 IM 07 – 07/03 DG 253/06 – HM – HIM HL MH Separated Assortments 78-II/AMIS – Sudanese mission.
53 IM 07 – 07/03 DG 261/06 – HM – HIM HL MH Separated Assortments 78-II/AMIS – Sudanese mission.
54 IM 07 – 07/03 DG 271/06 – HM – HIM HL MH Separated Assortments 80/AMIS - Sudanese mission; IM 07 – 07/03 DG 304/06 – HM – HIM HL MH Separated Assortments 80/AMIS – Sudanese mission.
55 Monthly Report EUSR Sudan. April 2006 - HM – HIM HL MH Separated Assortments 78-II/AMIS – Sudanese mission.
56 AU request for advisor's PSD/DITF/NV/1869 – HM – HIM HL- MH Separated Assortments 75/AMIS – Sudanese mission.
57 Draft Concept for EU Civilian/Military Supporting Action to AMIS II – HM – HIM HL MH Separated Assortments 78-I/AMIS - Sudanese mission.
58 IM 07 – 07/03 DG 315/06 – HM – HIM HL MH Separated Assortments 78-II/AMIS – Sudanese mission.
59 IM 07 – 07/03 DG 383/06 – HM – HIM HL MH Separated Assortments 78-II/AMIS – Sudanese mission.
60 EUSR MA weekly report – Week 06/2007 - HM – HIM HL MH Separated Assortments, 78-II/AMIS – Sudanese mission.
61 EU MSR weekly report – Week 04/2007 - HM – HIM HL MH Separated Assortments, 78-II/AMIS – Sudanese mission.
62 EU MSR weekly report – Week 21/2007 - HM – HIM HL MH Separated Assortments, 78-II/AMIS – Sudanese mission.
63 EU MSR weekly report – Week 23/2007 – HM – HIM HL MH Separated Assortments, 78-II/AMIS – Sudanese mission.
64 EU MSR weekly report – Week 26/2007 – HM – HIM HL MH Separated Assortments, 78-II/AMIS – Sudanese mission.
65 DGEUMS visit to Sudan/Darfur 18–20 June 2007 – HM – HIM HL MH Separated Assortments, 78-I/AMIS – Sudanese mission.

Chapter 6

1 The leadership of the EU was very pleased for the Hungarians to take part in the mission.
2 PSC meeting memorandum, 06. July 2004. - HM-HIM HL MH Separated Assortments, 79/AMIS – Sudanese mission.
3 Official Note: Hungarian Government and NGO support to Darfur, 08. September 2004. - HM-HIM HL MH Separated Assortments, 79/AMIS – Sudanese mission.
4 Designation of Hungarian Point of Contact, 207/PSC/Fax/2004. - HM-HIM HL MH Separated Assortments, 79/AMIS – Sudanese mission.
5 Summary report of Major Ferenc Kajári, 21 March 2005.- HM-HIM HL MH Separated Assortments, 75/AMIS – Sudanese mission.
6 Summary report of Major Ferenc Kajári, 21 March 2005.- HM-HIM HL MH Separated Assortments, 75/AMIS – Sudanese mission.
7 Summary report of Major Ferenc Kajári, 21 March 2005.- HM-HIM HL MH Separated Assortments, 75/AMIS – Sudanese mission.
8 Extension of our Hungarian military observer presence in Sudan, 230/PSC/EM/05, 27. April 2005. - HM-HIM HL MH Separated Assortments, 79/AMIS – Sudanese mission.
9 Summary report of Major Ferenc Kajári, 21 March 2005.- HM-HIM HL MH Separated Assortments, 75/AMIS – Sudanese mission and Besenyő (2016), pp. 208–110.
10 Summary report of Major Ferenc Kajári, 21 March 2005.- HM-HIM HL MH Separated Assortments, 75/AMIS – Sudanese mission.
11 Besenyő (2006), pp. 41–59.
12 74-4/ 157 /2005/EU - HM-HIM HL MH Separated Assortments, 79/AMIS – Sudanese mission.
13 HIM HL MH Separated Assortments, 76/AMIS – Sudanese mission.
14 Henry Kwami Anyidoho, *Guns Over Kigali: The Rwandese Civil War-1994. A Personal Account* (Accra: Woeli Publishing Services, 1997), p. 113.
15 AMIS II Movement Update - 24 August 2005 - HM-HIM HL MH Separated Assortments, 77/AMIS – Sudanese mission.
16 Colonel János Besenyő's unpublished diary of Darfur (2005), p. 43.
17 The other author of this book, Zsolt Szabó – when he was in Kuwait on a scholarship – had sometimes similar experiences, but the Arab people were more friendly and less suspicious compared to the Africans according to the account of Besenyő.
18 At the beginning of the AU, its first mission was in Burundi but without South African financial support, the UN had to take over. Emma Svenson, *The African mission in Burundi, Lessons Learned from the African Union's first peace operation,* FOI-R-2561-SE. Stockholm, 2008.
19 AMIS II Movement Update - 24 August 2005 - HM-HIM HL MH Separated Assortments, 77/AMIS – Sudanese mission; Besenyő (2016), pp. 115–116.
20 Colonel János Besenyő's unpublished diary (2005), p. 54.
21 Kőműves Kelemen (Clement Mason) is the name of a protagonist from a Hungarian ballad (and also the title of the work) from the sixteenth century. He is building a castle, but it keeps falling apart, so he builds his wife's body parts into the mortar so the castle will stand.
22 Colonel János Besenyő's unpublished diary (2005), p. 57.
23 Report on Darfur airlift, 25 October 2005. - HM-HIM HL MH Separated Assortments, 77/AMIS – Sudanese mission.
24 János Besenyő, 'First military operation between European Union and African Union. The European Advisors role in Darfur (AMIS)', *AARMS.* vol. 6, issue 4 (2007), http://real.mtak.hu/83791/1/18bese.pdf, accessed 22 March 2023.; Besenyő (2006).
25 Colonel János Besenyő's unpublished diary (2005), p. 40.
26 NATO Military Liaison Team in Addis Ababa – Weekly Sitrep 31/07, covering period 25 - 31 July 2007 - HM-HIM HL MH Separated Assortments, 78-I/AMIS – Sudanese mission.
27 Colonel János Besenyő's unpublished diary (2005), p. 83.
28 PSD/DITF/NV/030 - HM-HIM HL MH Separated Assortments, 80/AMIS – Sudanese mission.
29 Colonel János Besenyő's unpublished diary (2005), p. 85.
30 IM 07-07/03 DG 397/06 - HM-HIM HL MH Separated Assortments, 78-I/AMIS – Sudanese mission.
31 Besenyő (2007).; Besenyő (2006).
32 EUSR MA weekly report – Week 20/2007 - HM-HIM HL MH Separated Assortments, 78-II/AMIS – Sudanese mission.
33 Besenyő (2007).; Besenyő (2006).
34 Colonel János Besenyő's unpublished diary (2005), p. 59.
35 Besenyő (2007); Besenyő (2006).
36 Besenyő (2007); Besenyő (2006).
37 Besenyő (2007); Besenyő (2006).
38 AMIS II mission, 3/353/2005 HM-HVKFH, 25. November 2005. - HM-HIM HL MH Separated Assortments, 78-I/AMIS – Sudanese mission.
39 On 07 June 2006 and on 03 July 2006, but both were repulsed. Manning of the FJMHQ (IM 07-07/03 DG 348/06 - HM-HIM HL MH Separated

Assortments, 79/AMIS – Sudanese mission; FJMHQ AMIS (IM 07-07/03 DG 347/06 - HM-HIM HL MH Separated Assortments, 79/AMIS – Sudanese mission; EU Observer for the Ceasefire Commission in Sudan/Darfur (IM 07-07/03 DG 396/06 - HM-HIM HL MH Separated Assortments, 79/AMIS – Sudanese mission.

Chapter 7

1 Hastrup, pp. 34–36; Flint (2004).
2 Besenyő (2016) pp. 26–27.
3 PCS/AHG/Comm – 27.05. 2004. - HM-HIM HL MH Separated Assortments, 75/AMIS – Sudanese mission.
4 Great Britain: Parliament: House of Commons, International Development Committee, *Darfur: The Killing Continues; Second Report of Session 2005-06; Report, Together with Formal Minutes, Oral and Written Evidence,* The Stationery Office, 2006, pp. 6–7.; Anon. (2007).
5 Besenyő (2006, pp. 41–59.
6 African Union, *The African Union and the conflict in the Darfur region of the Sudan. Meeting the challenges of peace, security and stability, CONF/PLG/3(I).* Addis Ababa, 2005, https://reliefweb.int/sites/reliefweb.int/files/resources/A0AD919C2B396D0FC125700D004A49AC-au-afr-26may.pdf accessed 25 March 2023.
7 János Besenyő, 'EU Support to the African Union Mission in Darfur – AMIS', *Tradecraft Review, Periodical of the Scientific Board of Military Security Office,* Special Issue (2009), http://dx.doi.org/10.2139/ssrn.3610699, accessed 25 March 2023.
8 Anon. (2007).
9 Seth Appiah-Mensah, 'The African Mission in Sudan: Darfur dilemmas', *African Security Studies*, vol. 15, issue 1 (2006), 1–19.
10 Anon. (2005).
11 Anon. (2006).
12 Besenyő interviewed officers in 2007, and according to them the operation was almost completely led by the UN and the EU. Appiah-Mensah, pp. 1–19.
13 UN Security Council, *Belgium, Congo, France, Italy, Peru, Slovakia and United Kingdom of Great Britain and Northern Ireland: draft resolution S/2007/468*, 2007, https://digitallibrary.un.org/record/604362 accessed 25 March 2023.
14 DGEUMS visit to Sudan/Darfur 18–20 June 2007 - HM-HIM HL MH Separated Assortments, 78-I/AMIS – Sudanese mission.
15 Besenyő (2016), pp. 79–80.
16 Coleman and Williams (2017).
17 EU Organisation Arrangements to Manage the Consolidated Package of Support to AMIS II - HM-HIM HL MH Separated Assortments, 78-I/AMIS – Sudanese mission.
18 PSC meeting .03.06.2004 - HM-HIM HL MH Special Collection Documents, 80 / AMIS - Sudan mission; Fact Sheet: EU Response to the Crisis in Darfur, Brussels, 10th June 2004 - HM-HIM HL MH Separated Assortments, 78-II/AMIS – Sudanese mission.
19 PSC meeting .03.06.2004 - HM-HIM HL MH Separated Assortments, 80/AMIS – Sudanese mission; EU meeting of AMIS deployed EU MILOBs and technical planning experts, IM 07-07/03 DG 188/05 - HM-HIM HL MH Separated Assortments, 80/AMIS – Sudanese mission.
20 Draft Council Conclusions - Sudan/Darfur, Brussels, 27 October 2004 - HM-HIM HL MH Separated Assortments, 78-II/AMIS – Sudanese mission.
21 Information Paper on possible EU military implications in the light of the Action Plan for ESDP support to Peace and Security in Africa, IM 01-16/20-07 OPS 212/04. - HM-HIM HL MH Separated Assortments, 78-II/AMIS – Sudanese mission.
22 Press Information - Javier Solana, EU High Representative for the CFSP, to meet with the Chairman of the African Union Commission Alpha Oumar Konare, Tuesday 17 May 2005 - HM-HIM HL MH Separated Assortments, 80/AMIS – Sudanese mission.
23 NATO Military Liaison Team in Addis Ababa – Weekly Sitrep 16/07, covering period 12 – 20 April 2007 - HM-HIM HL MH Separated Assortments, 80/AMIS – Sudanese mission.
24 Information Note to the Political and Security Committee (PSC) on the Requirement to Amend the 3rd Contribution Agreement with the African Union (AU) on the Financing of the AMIS Operation in Darfur from the African Peace Facility (APF); PSD/DITF/NV/1365 - HM-HIM HL MH Separated Assortments, 80/AMIS – Sudanese mission.
25 IM 07-07/07 OPS 112/05 - HM-HIM HL MH Separated Assortments, 78-I/AMIS – Sudanese mission.
26 Besenyő (2006).
27 EU Organisation Arrangements to Manage the Consolidated Package of Support to AMIS II - HM-HIM HL MH Separated Assortments, 78-II/AMIS – Sudanese mission; Draft Concept for EU Civilian/Military Supporting Action to AMIS II - HM-HIM HL MH Separated Assortments, 78-II/AMIS – Sudanese mission.
28 EU meeting of AMIS deployed EU MILOBs and technical planning experts, IM 07-07/03 DG 188/05 - HM-HIM HL MH Separated Assortments, 80/AMIS – Sudanese mission; Report: Council Secretariat AMIS II assessment mission 16-22 September 2005 – HM-HIM HL MH Separated Assortments, 78-II/AMIS – Sudanese mission.
29 Besenyő (2007), pp. 771–784.
30 HM-HIM HL MH Separated Assortments, 75/AMIS – Sudanese mission.

ABOUT THE AUTHORS

Col. (Ret.) János Besenyő is a professor in Óbuda University (Hungary) and head of the Africa Research Institute. Between 1987 and 2018, he worked as a professional soldier and served in several peace operations in Africa and Afghanistan. He received a PhD in military science from Zrínyi Miklós National Defence University and a habilitated doctorate at Eötvös Lóránd University. In 2014, he established the Scientific Research Center of the Hungarian Defence Forces General Staff and was its first leader from 2014 to 2018. His most recent publication is Darfur Peacekeepers: The African Union Peacekeeping Mission in Darfur (AMIS) from the Perspective of a Hungarian Military Advisor.

Zsolt Szabó is a PhD-aspirant at Eszterházy Károly Catholic University and junior researcher at the Africa Research Institute at Óbuda University, Doctoral School for Safety and Security Sciences. He has published articles and reviews in several journal. After finishing his PhD, he would like to continue researching African security politics in the frame of the institution.